INSPIRE
COURAGE

INSPIRE COURAGE

Inspiring Writings about Courage

ANTHOLOGY 2022

Edited by
DEBRA CELOVSKY
and
ROBYNNE ELIZABETH MILLER

INSPIRE COURAGE

Copyright © 2022 Inspire Christian Writers. Individual pieces within this anthology are copyrights of the authors.

All rights reserved. No part of this publication may be reproduced, distributed, translated, or transmitted in any form or by any means, including photocopying, recording, or other electronic or mechanical methods, without the prior written permission of the author, except in the case of brief quotations embodied in critical reviews and certain other noncommercial uses permitted by copyright law.

ISBN 978-1-938196-21-8

Scripture quotations marked (ESV) are taken from The ESV® Bible (The Holy Bible, English Standard Version®), copyright © 2001 by Crossway, a publishing ministry of Good News Publishers. Used by permission. All rights reserved.

Scripture quotations marked HCSB are taken from the Holman Christian Standard Bible®, Used by Permission HCSB ©1999, 2000, 2002, 2003, 2009 Holman Bible Publishers. Holman Christian Standard Bible®, Holman CSB®, and HCSB® are federally registered trademarks of Holman Bible Publishers.

Scripture quotations marked (ICB) are taken from the International Children's Bible®. Copyright © 1986, 1988, 1999 by Thomas Nelson. Used by permission. All rights reserved.

Scripture quotations marked (NASB) are taken from the (NASB®) New American Standard Bible®, Copyright © 1960, 1971, 1977, 1995, 2020 by The Lockman Foundation. Used by permission. All rights reserved. www.lockman.org

Scripture quotations marked (NIV) are taken from the Holy Bible, New International Version®, NIV®. Copyright © 1973, 1978, 1984, 2011 by Biblica, Inc.™ Used by permission of Zondervan. All rights reserved worldwide. www.zondervan.com. The "NIV" and "New International Version" are trademarks registered in the United States Patent and Trademark Office by Biblica, Inc.™

Scripture quotations marked (NKJV) are taken from the New King James Version®. Copyright © 1982 by Thomas Nelson. Used by permission. All rights reserved.

Cover designed by Lainey La Shay
Interior design & layout by Author Digital Services
Published by Inspire Christian Writers

Dedication

This anthology is dedicated to those who have shown courage or have witnessed it firsthand ... courage to speak boldly, walk through grief and loss, ask forgiveness, and take steps of faith. This bravery gives witness to the hope and strength we find in Jesus.

This collection is also dedicated to the writers of Inspire, whose bravery in sharing their stories means we get a first-row seat to what God has done, and continues to do ... and to be encouraged as we walk through whatever challenges we face.

Have I not commanded you? Be strong and courageous.
Do not be frightened, and do not be dismayed, for the
LORD your God is with you wherever you go
(Josh. 1:9, ESV).

Special thanks to:

Debra Celovsky

Robynne E. Miller

Ian Feavearyear

The entire editorial team

(What an honor to work with you all!)

Lainey La Shay, cover artist extraordinaire

And the board of directors of Inspire Christian Writers

Without all of you, this project

would never have happened.

Thank you.

Contents

Introduction | 1

1. The World in One Word
   by Joyce Dixon Hightower 3
2. You Are So Brave!
   by Robyn Mulder 11
3. Courage Through Christ
   by Janet M. Barr 15
4. Courage vs. Recklessness
   by Malcolm Mackinnon 19
5. When All Other Lights Go Out
   by Lainey La Shay 27
6. Courage to Embrace My Calling
   by Margaux Krause 35
7. We Do Not Trust in Horses—or Mules
   by Anita Peluso 45
8. The Minister's Daughter, Hard Exit
   by Elain Juliusson 49
9. One Tiny Step
   by Terrie Hellard-Brown 57
10. "With-You" Courage
    by Damon J. Gray 59
11. Once More Unto the Breach
    by Christine Hagion 67
12. Learning Courage
    by Heather Popish 75
13. The Bravest Girl
    by Robynne Elizabeth Miller 77
14. Finding Courage
    by D.H. Weinberg 85

15	Terror and the Paper Bags by Karen D. Wood	93
16	Courage, COVID, and Standing Up for Christ by Carlitta Cole-Kelly	101
17	Adventure is on the Other Side of Fear by Darcy Schock	109
18	In My Eyes by Heather Popish	117
19	Moonlight Kisses by Michele Marie Weisman	119
20	Under One Condition by Libby Taylor-Worden	125
21	Courage vs. Wisdom by Malcolm Mackinnon	131
22	God, Courage, and Toilet Paper by Debbie Jones Warren	139
23	The Doors by Lenette Lindsey	147
24	When the Itsy Bitsy Spider Isn't by Debra Celovsky	155
25	The Courage to Share by Rebecca Mitchell	159
26	Courageous Love by Kimberly Novak	167
27	Born First of Love by Janelle Roselli	173

Index of Authors | *177*
Meet the Authors | *179*
About Inspire Christian Writers | *189*

INSPIRE
COURAGE

Introduction

Although the world has certainly opened up in the last year or so, it's also true that we've just walked through one of the most uncertain and concerning periods in recent memory. And much has changed in that time.

From the way we check out at stores to the decisions we make regarding vacations, events, and gatherings, things have most definitely changed. For just about all of us.

Some of that change has been imposed as the world tried to minimize the effects of a global pandemic and figure out the safest and most effective response. Some change was forged via our own beliefs based on information we've received, evidence we've considered, and personal convictions. And, sometimes, our choices were tinged with fear … for our communities, families, and ourselves.

But 2 Timothy, 1:7, reminds us that "God gave us a spirit not of fear but of power and love and self-control (ESV)." This Scripture is a reminder most of us have needed in the last few years.

While the church, as a whole, had varied responses, recent events has allowed a core belief to re-emerge and assert itself: however we, as Christians, conduct ourselves, whether in the midst of a global health crisis or in facing our own personal fears, Jesus wants to walk with us.

We hope this anthology, a collection of stories, articles, and poems about the many facets of courage, reminds you of the many ways we can be brave. More than that, we hope every word in this book points you back to the reason we can walk through any challenge with confidence: Jesus.

– 1 –

The World in One Word
Joyce Dixon Hightower

After a grueling eight-hour ride in the back of a wooden flatbed truck over rocky, unpaved roads, we had arrived. We descended to the small town of Moyale at the border between Kenya and Ethiopia. As a college senior in an international program, I was living on a student's budget. I had joined some students hitchhiking around East Africa during a two-week school break. Bruised and shaken to the bone by the ride, not one of us protested the decision to pay for a stay at the only hotel in town.

Early the next morning, needing to buy bottled water to brush my teeth and to drink, I ran to the small shop across the dirt road. Normally, I could point at what I wanted on a store shelf but saw no visible water. Having learned some Swahili, I said the word for water to the shop owner. He stared at me as if waiting for me to continue.

He replied, "What water?"

I searched the shop walls, confirming no example to point to. So, I repeated the word and he repeated his reply.

He muttered impatiently and called out, "Pili!"

A boy dressed in a school uniform playing outside answered immediately and dashed into the shop. The shopkeeper said something which sent Pili running like lightning. He returned in a few minutes with a man.

After speaking in Swahili to the shop owner, the man turned to me and spoke in perfect English, calmly and politely, "Hello, my name is Albert, the school headmaster. Issa, the owner, sent for me. Can I help you?"

"Oh, thank you, Albert. I'm Eva. I'm telling Issa I want water, 'moja'."

"I see." He frowned, then turned to explain to Issa.

Throwing his hands up, Issa shook his head. He reached under the counter and retrieved two different-sized bottles of water, placed them on the counter, and gestured for me to choose. I pointed to the larger one.

"Shilingi nne," Issa said.

"That will cost four shillings," Albert translated.

Issa was frowning and tight-lipped. His voice was raised as he spoke to Albert while he took my money and gave me change.

"What did he say? Did I do something wrong?" I asked.

"He said to tell you that 'moja' means 'one' in Swahili. You asked for 'one.' He kept asking 'one of what?' The word 'maji' means 'water.' You confused the words. Issa says that you should be careful because one word can open a door to a new world."

"Oh, my goodness. Yes, that's right, I mixed up the words. Tell Issa how sorry I am for the trouble and I'm grateful for his patience. Thank you for your help, Albert." Taking the bottle, I waved goodbye to Issa and Pili and headed back to the hotel.

"Hello, could I talk with you a minute?" Albert called, running across the street to catch up with me. "How did you arrive?"

"I am with a group of hitchhiking college students."

He was delighted and wanted to talk to us all. I ran and convinced my friends to come and listen to him, out of respect for his position. During our discussion over breakfast, Albert asked a lot of questions, although he wasn't clear about why. Finally, saying he risked being late to start school, he asked us to meet him again at dinner.

We explained that, as hitchhikers, we had to be ready to leave at a moment's notice. He assured us that the next truck would not arrive for two days because vehicles crossing the border only went on days when there was a lot of traffic and armed guards. This security was to avoid being targeted by the Shifta bandits who lived in the mountains surrounding certain parts of the road. The news dampened our spirits, but we agreed to meet that evening.

By the end of dinner Albert had made a passionate request for me to take two years out of my plans to go to medical school and spend it teaching high school science there. These two years would help students become strong enough in the sciences to qualify for further studies. They could then go to medical school and serve their countrymen. The scale was tipped when he promised that by doing so, I would change the course of the country's history.

Eight months later, with my degree and some saved money in hand, I was ready. That week, terrible news came from Albert. The town, including the school, had been burned down, with shops raided and a few people killed by Shifta bandits. Albert promised to find another school. Soon afterward he wrote he had located a school and to come immediately. On arrival, however, the promised position was no longer available. Discouraged and at the point of leaving, I was then presented with another position by a local pastor.

This school had been built in a rural area by a community of poor farmers who then sent their children for education with the hope of a better future. Unfortunately, it was not a hope the students shared. They expected little from themselves and their lives after not showing a score in scholastic aptitude high enough to get into a secondary government school. The girls explained they needed to complete the four years to get good husbands willing to pay high "bride" prices. The boys needed to complete the four years to get a job that provided enough income to build an acceptable two-room shelter, buy a wife, and provide food for their expected family. No one was interested in going more than twenty-five miles away or getting a higher education.

This stunned me. I had come halfway around the world to help students become medical professionals, only to find these students did not want help. If I mentioned they could use something in future studies, eyes would roll.

One day a student decided I was pushing too hard and angrily called out in the middle of class: "Do you know this is a community-built school? Do you see the dirt floors and the windows with no glass? We study at night by candlelight, because there aren't enough lanterns. A generator is unthinkable. Our parents are pretending we are doing something significant in a building they don't have the money to finish. You are the only qualified teacher to ever work here because the government pays your salary. How can you imagine that anything will change? Please, let us pass these two remaining years in peace. *Hakuna matumaini*: There is no hope."

That harpoon of discouragement struck deep into my heart's soft flesh. I swallowed hard, trying to fight back tears. I was almost overwhelmed by the deadly poison of hopelessness released by their words as they tried to wedge their way through the harpoon's gaping wound into the seat of my faith. *Had I wasted my time, hope, and money to come all this way for nothing? Where was the confirmation God had given me? Was this a mistake?*

No! I screamed internally. I refused to accept defeat. I would not give up. I could either fight my hardest or just go home. I chose to believe the impossible could happen.

I looked up as the class sat quiet and motionless.

Clearing my throat, I crossed my arms and took a deep breath. "All right. Some agree with the words spoken. *Hakuna matumaini*: There is no hope. What she meant was *Hatuna matumaini*: We have no hope. One letter changes the meaning of the word. One word opened the door for me to stand here today. I believe things can change, but I can't force you to believe it. That faith … that desire … must come from deep inside you. There's hope in some of you or God would not have sent me here. Anyone wanting to try for a government school scholarship after this, tell me during tonight's study period." I was disabled by heartache and assigned reading for the remaining time.

* * *

My heart still ached that evening in the silence of the study period. At the bell, students hurried to the dormitories except for four young men sitting in the far corner.

"Gentlemen, why are you not hurrying to bed? The last bell is soon."

"Teacher," Bundi said, leading the others forward. "We want to try … to see if what you said can be true."

They stood there grinning expectantly, and my heart soared with healing hope.

Joyce Dixon Hightower

Extra hard work and prayer for these four students brought amazing results. After two years, they received scholarships for further education and national recognition. Students at other community schools aspired to break down barriers of unbelief and let hope enter. Kenya would have four more medical doctors and the hope for more. Courageous perseverance had awakened the power of hope and faith that lies deep inside each of us.

Issa was right again. One word can open the door to a new world.

-2-
You Are So Brave!
Robyn Mulder

"You are so brave!"

My friend stepped closer and wrapped me in a strong hug.

I awkwardly hugged her back as tears ran down my cheeks. I didn't feel brave as we embraced. Life had separated us years earlier, but time fell away when we happened to meet up again at this youth event in the Colorado Rockies.

Several months earlier I had gone to the hospital for almost a week because of a major depressive episode. Hopelessness had almost gotten the best of me. I had been improving since I went home, but on this day — in spite of the beautiful mountains surrounding us — I was struggling. I missed my family. Needing to be upbeat with the students and leaders was taxing my still-fragile emotional health. I wondered why I had even applied to be on staff for this event.

When Cheryl saw me outside the auditorium, her face lit up as she greeted me. "Hi Robyn! How are you?"

I'm sure she didn't expect to see tears filling my eyes as I whimpered, "I'm not having a very good day."

She didn't reel back in shock and run away, embarrassed for both of us. Instead, she leaned in and said the perfect thing: "You are so brave!"

I don't even remember the rest of our conversation, but that simple phrase stuck with me. To this day it gives me courage when I most need it.

Many people live with a mental illness like anxiety or depression. That certainly requires courage, but we need to remember that everyone faces situations that demand bravery.

It takes courage to quit your job and stay home with your kids. It also takes courage to put your baby in daycare and go back to work.

You need determination when you get a cancer diagnosis. You also need determination when someone you love finds out they have cancer.

It takes guts to be assertive and tell your boss that something needs to change at work. It also takes guts to lovingly point out a problem in your relationship with your spouse.

You need bravery when you apply for a new job. You also need bravery when you decide to put in your two weeks' notice.

Life can be wonderful but, often, it's scary. Bad things do occur. No one has any guarantees about what will happen in the next five minutes, let alone the next five years.

All of us are brave in our own way, even if we don't think about the courage it takes to make certain choices. Some days are easier than others, but when someone deals with depression and anxiety it can feel impossible to face those fears and make even the simplest decisions. Some people need courage just to get out of bed and go through the routines of the day. It takes courage to decide to keep on living.

You usually don't know who is struggling with that. They're probably good at keeping those feelings hidden. Those are the people who need an extra dose of courage from the community around them. They need someone to really see them.

In a world where it often seems as if no one cares, it can be encouraging to connect with someone who looks you in the eye, really cares how you are when they ask, and makes the effort to let you know you matter.

Relating in that way may even give someone the nerve to be honest about how they're feeling.

As we walk through each day courageously facing all of life's challenges, let's keep our eyes open for the ones who are struggling. And when we catch a glimpse of their heroic quest to keep going despite their fears, let's never miss the opportunity to throw our arms around them and reassure them with four simple words:

"You are so brave!"

– 3 –

Courage Through Christ
Janet M. Barr

There's courage in her eyes and in her smile
As she regards the plight of someone else.
Though her own heavy burden stays the same,
She lifts another up, and casts herself
Upon the One who suffered patiently.
He trusted God. He answered wisely when
His enemies spat spite, and comforts cold
Surrounded Him, myopic-visioned friends.

Did *they* have any concept how the Man
Felt weary and alone while facing sin?

Janet M. Barr

His punishment, our cross, was borne in love,
He bravely drank the cup and entered in.

A travesty! Unfair! His life for ours —
A monstrous trade — Yet here's why she endures:
Though darkness had its day as Jesus died,
The resurrection promise was assured.

The God-Man's perfect life was sacrificed
So guilty, clueless ones could live. God's Lamb
Was cut, through purest white. Salvation's blood
Became her life, so she can say, *I am,*
Though devastated in these dreadful times,
With hope undone like death, by broken plans,
Still certain, He, who always, all ways wins,
Is holding me, no matter where I am.

Believing Christ, the Lamb, is her Supply,
Beholding Him, and life, with eyes like His,
Desiring to obey, to seek Him first,
She reads He's *faithful*, and she knows He is.

Her courage will be counted. Soon she'll be
With Christ, the Lamb *and* Lion of her days.

Her knees will bow and, face to face, her eyes
Will finally see the One who kept her brave.

– 4 –
Courage vs. Recklessness
Malcolm Mackinnon

There is a fine line between courage and recklessness. Courage is a virtue, something we would attribute to the noble. Recklessness, on the other hand, belongs in the domain of fools. How do we tell the difference? The difference lies in whether the cause of courage is worthy and God-approved.

For example, a father trying to rescue his young daughter from a mountain lion would be courageous. Not only would the cause be right and worthy, there would be a reasonable expectation of success, despite the probability of incurring some injury. However, if the same man, while driving through a safari park, stopped in the middle of a lion enclosure, then got out of the car to show his family how brave he was, we would classify him among the reckless rather than the courageous.

Faith in God requires the right kind of courage, and not the wrong kind. God's instruction is to trust Him, not to test Him.

The story of Jonathan in 1 Samuel 14 demonstrates the difference. At the beginning of the account, the Israelites were under severe oppression from the Philistines. The war had been going on for some time and the Philistines had the upper hand.

The Israelites were almost at the point of submission. They were hiding in caves, with no weapons, scared of the Philistines' power and dreading the imminent likelihood of becoming completely subjected to them. Only King Saul and Jonathan, his son, had swords. Jonathan also had an armor-bearer.

An atmosphere of defeat surrounded them. There was no hope, there was no future, and the promise of God's people thriving in the Promised Land had become a distant pipedream.

Yet, while everyone else waited for the inevitable surrender, Jonathan had different ideas. Amid the disaster, he still had the mindset to believe God might yet want to do something. Moreover, if that was the

Courage vs. Recklessness

case, he wanted to be the instrument through whom God would work.

We can't doubt his bravery. But, at first glance, his zeal seems unreasonable ... swinging more to the reckless side than the courageous. In addition, Jonathan didn't just wait until he was cornered and then fight his way out, which might have given him an opportunity to show his courage. Instead, he turned a passive idea into an active one. He decided to go and pick a fight with the Philistines.

As he contemplated launching an attack, he reasoned: *Perhaps the Lord will act in our behalf* (1 Sam. 14:6 NIV). He and his armor-bearer found themselves close to a Philistine outpost. Jonathan suggested they show themselves to the Philistines who happened to be at the top of a cliff. In Hebrew, the cliff's name means "slippery."

You don't have to be a military tactician to know it's a great disadvantage to attack an enemy from below. All the people at the top had to do was hurl down rocks and anything else they could lay their hands on. Jonathan had talked his armor-bearer into the plan and, for some strange reason, he wholeheartedly agreed with it. What on earth were they both thinking?

The outpost contained twenty Philistine warriors. All armed. All bored. All ready to have an excuse to kill some Israelites. Let's put this into perspective; two men with limited weaponry decided it would be a good idea to climb up a slippery cliff to start a fight with twenty soldiers waiting at the top for them. What could possibly go wrong?

At first, it seems we've not just entered a world of recklessness, but utter insanity. This no longer appears to be a man defending his daughter from a mountain lion. It now looks like a man who has stepped out of the car in the lion enclosure, locked the door, thrown away the keys, covered himself in raw meat, and started to throw stones at the lions!

People throwing their lives away in crazy quests are of no use to God. There is something compelling about witnessing a person who believes victory is possible when all others only see defeat. If the ambition fails, we are left shaking our heads sadly at their misplaced expectations. However, when the belief turns into a reality, the person can create inspiration in others like nothing else.

I remember a man like that. In 1981, England hosted Australia in a five-day cricket test match. In these games, both teams have two innings. Australia scored 401 runs in their first innings against England's score of 174. In the second innings, England had scored 135 with only three of their ten batters left. They were still

Courage vs. Recklessness

92 behind and Australia still had their entire second innings to come. Defeat was so sure, the bookmakers at the ground gave England odds of 500 to 1 against winning the game.

One of the remaining batters was Ian Botham. Somehow, he had forgotten to read the script. Amid the prospect of certain defeat, he alone retained the strange idea that England could still win. So, he started to bat ferociously, hitting the ball to every part of the ground. However, he did it with skill and not just with wild abandonment. Slowly, his impact became infectious. First, the crowd started to cultivate hope, not in any kind of victory, but just that someone was willing to stand up and fight. Then, his teammates adopted a similar attitude. They batted so well, they surpassed the Australian score, and forced them to have to bat again.

Even then, the target for Australia was only 130. Everybody knew they would reach it without much fuss. But what Botham had done was galvanize the rest of his teammates to believe. And belief is a very powerful thing. The team rose to the occasion, fighting for each other, and restricted the Australians to only 111. England won the match and launched a new era of success. All because one man had faith that victory was possible.

Was Botham courageous or reckless? It could be argued he took a few chances and rode his luck. But what was there to lose? It wasn't a matter of life or death. I prefer to think he showed courage, retaining a mindset which insisted on persevering and not giving up, even when everyone else had.

Similarly, Jonathan refused to concede. And, contrary to first appearances, Jonathan was *not* reckless. He knew what the power of God with him could achieve. He would have known about the exploits of Samson and so many others who stepped out in courageous faith to allow God to work on their behalf.

But even knowing what God could do, Jonathan still did not embark on his quest until he had the absolute assurance of God's approval. Therefore, before he took one step, he set out a fleece. He asked the Lord for the men to say a particular sentence, indicating they wanted Jonathan to come up to them. In turn, this would be the indication to Jonathan that God would fight for them.

The men said the exact sentence to show God had given them into his hands. Now, here's the courage: when God gives the green light, we then have to step out in faith and do what we said we were going to do.

And Jonathan did so. He and his armor-bearer climbed the cliff and defeated every one of the twenty

Courage vs. Recklessness

Philistines. Not only did they win a great victory on behalf of Israel, the news of the triumph spread quickly. The Israelites came out of their caves and holes in the ground with a new national fervor. The reminder that God was on their side transformed them and, on that day, the balance of the war changed. The Israelites went from oppressed to oppressors, and hunted down the Philistines who had not only opposed them but also the God they served.

God calls us to be courageous. Our courage is shown in holding our position, being prepared to uphold the Word of God, giving an account of what we believe, and standing up for right in a world of wrong. But God also reminds us to distinguish between courage and recklessness.

Jonathan sets before us a wonderful pattern of Godly courage. We see his desire to do something for God. He helps us to believe God might want to use us. He reminds us that nothing hinders our God from saving, whether by many or few. He encourages us to bring our ideas to God, and to wait for the confirmation of His approval. And, he inspires us to set out in faith and courage, knowing our God fights our battles for us.

– 5 –
When All Other Lights Go Out
Lainey La Shay

We're half a mile underground when the far wall of the cavern disappears.

"Karl, my headlamp is going out!" A pang of fear rushes through me. Heat burns its way to my ears despite the freezing temperatures in the damp cave.

He stops mid-step over a crevasse half as wide as he is tall. As he returns to my side, the beam of his headlamp dazzles my eyes, creating a confetti of light. "Are you sure?"

"Positive." Three minutes ago, the black basalt with its swirl of earthy reds, grays, and whites was visible under the broad beam of my headlamp. A waterfall trickled down under the volcanic rock. Stalactites clung to the lava tube's ceiling a hundred feet above our heads. Stalagmites rose up from the cavern floor toward them, stretching their fingertips toward each other, reaching but never touching.

Now all of it is veiled in a shroud of darkness.

I give the headlamp a good thump.

"Here, love, I have batteries." Karl shrugs out of his crimson Patagonia backpack and kneels to rummage through its contents. Snacks, spare clothes, bike locks, a fuzzy moose hat—if anyone is prepared for this, it's the man I'm dating. But his brow furrows. "*You* don't happen to have the batteries, do you?"

My cell phone provides the extra light I need to dig through my backpack. Even if I don't find the package of AA batteries, at least I have a spare flashlight. *Right?* My wide eyes meet Karl's, and I press a hand to the top of my forehead. "I don't have anything."

Sitting back on my heels, I chew my lower lip that's already chapped from the desert heat outside. I rake through my memories. Where did we leave them?

On the dashboard. In the car. A half-mile and more than an hour back the way we came. We're thirty miles from anywhere in the middle of Coconino National Forest. We'll never find our way out of here without decent light, and it could be a week before another hiker ventures deep enough into the lava tube to fish us out.

As we descended into the gaping maw of the cave system, we had passed a handful of people retreating from their depths. They had scrambled up a steep incline of slick, wet boulders as if a mythical creature were chasing them. "Not for us!" a woman exclaimed.

"Dad had a panic attack down there," one kid announced.

The dad clambered up the forty-five-degree slope on all fours, too concerned with getting to the light to worry about his ego.

Despite the fear written on their pale faces, Karl and I charged forward, sliding down the boulders on our backsides to avoid losing balance or twisting an ankle. When the subterranean trail leveled out, an eighth of a mile down, we were alone and we hadn't seen a soul since.

I zip my jacket up to my chin and tug my chunky knit hat around my ears. It's my "lucky" hat, given to me by my six-year-old nephew. But I'm not feeling so lucky today.

Tears swell in my eyes. I choke them back. We should make tracks for the entrance, but my feet are welded to the ground. I'm tired of being brave, and I'm done with slamming into obstacles at every turn. Our visit to the lava caves feels ironic. The entire last year has felt like we've been wandering through Earth's deepest, darkest places. We had faced domestic violence threats from former family, had to cope with the grief of a suicide, and had moved across the country.

Some days it felt as if there was no hope, that all the light had gone out from the world. We felt our way through each day, and some days, we stumbled and fell. Somehow, we got back up and kept looking for the light.

Which is why we are here in Flagstaff in the first place—looking for some calm in the storm. But this isn't exactly what I had in mind.

"Dear God, what do we do now?" My whisper fades into the silence.

"Lainey, look!" Karl hands me a spare headlamp that he's pulled from a side pocket. "I have an extra. I didn't even know I owned a second one."

My thumb punches the button, and the basalt illuminates in front of me. A quiver ripples through my body. Tears fall from relief. "Thank you, Jesus!"

Karl wipes my tears away and kisses my forehead. "You know, we're almost to the end of the tunnel. What do you say we try for it?"

"Only if you're sure these other lights won't run out of batteries."

He grins. "No promises."

"If we get stuck down here, I'm going to feed you to the dragon." I hoist my backpack, poking him in the rib as I march past.

"Wait, you didn't tell me there was a dragon!" Karl laughs and quickens his stride to fall in step beside me. He reaches out, fingers brushing against mine, and gives my hand three squeezes. *I love you*.

We pick our way over gaping cracks and crumbling stones. Once flowing red-hot, ripples of lava are now frozen in time beneath our boots. The flap of a bat's wing rustles past my ear, stirring the otherwise still air against my cheek.

The ceiling lowers until we have to crouch. We're both on our hands and knees within fifteen feet, then slithering on our bellies to make it through the narrow tunnel section.

A bead of sweat trickles down my back. What if there's an earthquake? We are in an active volcanic field, after all. What if these old tunnels lose their strength and collapse? We'd be lost in this black labyrinth forever.

My courage almost fails until Karl reaches his hand back for mine. He pulls me to my feet next to him as the path widens and continues. He's calm and collected, the thrill of adventure invigorating him. I wish that were me, but the weight of last year's heartbreak makes it hard to be.

Water trickles through the cave ahead of us, drip-drip-dripping in the distance. We follow the sound until the tunnel comes to an abrupt end. It had been sealed off millennia ago when the volcanic eruption that formed it ceased.

"Let's turn off our headlamps," Karl suggests. His blue eyes spark with the orneriness of a kid presenting a wild dare.

Here's my chance to let the thrill of the adventure carry me away. How I want to let it! But what if the lights don't turn back on?

"Come on, love. Where's that courage I know you have?"

A sniff of resignation rises out of me. My palms dig into my hips, and I shift my weight. "Fine. Two minutes. Not a second more."

"Two minutes." Karl draws an "x" over his heart. "Promise."

We cozy up on a boulder, and I sigh as I study the ceiling. "Life with you is such an adventure." I look at him and wrap his hand in mine. "But I wouldn't change a thing."

His smile melts my heart. "Okay. Ready?"

"Ready."

When All Other Lights Go Out

"One. Two. Three!"

We click off our headlamps and plunge into the night.

The physical weight of darkness had been unrecognizable to me before. Now, pressure wraps tight around me, crushing my ribs and squeezing the breath from my lungs. My heart fights back, racing twice as fast to keep it all at bay.

My ears strain to hear something, anything, in the silence. My heart drums a frenetic beat. Something scurries to my right, its four feet tapping against the wet lava. A pair of bats flap their wings hard as they give chase. A ragged sound reaches my ears. Is that … a dragon? No, it's my own breathing.

Flashes and figures dance before my eyes as they try to make out some semblance of shape in the complete blackness. Scenes from the last year play out in living color in front of my eyes, gaining traction the longer the lights remain doused.

Just like this lava tube, Karl and I walked through those dark days together, hand in hand. Even when things were most uncertain, both of us on the verge of falling apart and crippled with fear, there was still hope. Hope was the light we clung to when all other lights went out.

Even here, a mile underground, there was still hope. The climb back to the surface would be exhausting, but the sun would be waiting in the same way a brighter future was waiting for us.

Karl's lamp flared back to life. He wrapped his arm around my shoulders and pulled me close against his warm body. I fit perfectly against his ribs. He kissed the top of my head and whispered, "You're the bravest woman I know. We'll get through this."

My lips curl into a smile. "You can count on it."

– 6 –
Courage to Embrace My Calling

Margaux Krause

For years I dreamed of quitting my job and leaving my cubicle to impact people's lives more directly. But when I finally had an opportunity to influence my children as a stay-at-home mom, I feared giving up work.

This reflection highlights the biblical encouragement from friends that led me to courageously embrace God's calling to stay-at-home motherhood. Further, my story connects to the days of Ezra when God gave the people of Judah courage to rebuild His temple in Jerusalem.

Margaux Krause

Called to Serve

> We are the servants of the God of heaven and earth … (Ezra 5:11 NIV).

God impressed upon me the desire to serve my family as a stay-at-home mom when my first daughter was born. Although I had the option of returning part-time, I chose to work full-time and let daycare change my daughter's diapers. But seeing photos of my daughter at daycare made me deeply regret taking the easy way out.

While expecting our second child, my desire to stay home from work skyrocketed. Unfortunately, halfway through the pregnancy I experienced an unexpected miscarriage leading to the tragic loss of our son. I struggled to trust that God was saying, *you can quit, but not yet.*

When our next child on earth finally arrived, her sweet birth clearly marked the time for me to quit working. After maternity leave, I unleashed the difficult news to my boss by trusting that God was calling me to full-time motherhood.

In the Book of Ezra, God called the people of Judah to return into His service at Jerusalem. With royal fanfare, King Cyrus proclaimed surviving Jews could leave exile in Babylon to rebuild the temple in their holy land. At first, the Jews' release from captivity seemed simple, just like putting in my two weeks' notice was a straightforward step.

Afraid to Go On

> Then the people around them set out to discourage the people of Judah and make them afraid to go on building (Ezra 4:4 NIV).

Looking back, I believe the Enemy tried to prevent me from choosing full-time motherhood by playing into my fears of giving up career life. Evidently, there are no promotions, performance bonuses, or days off for moms.

Hardly twenty-four hours following my last day of work, other employers started knocking at my door with work-from-home options. Over a few months I answered phone interviews, sent job proposals, and formed an LLC business. I squeezed all this hubbub in between nursing my newborn and potty training my toddler, distracted from serving them wholeheartedly.

When temple rebuilding began, enemies in the land worried this act would restore governing power to the people of Judah. So, these enemies sought to suppress and instill fear in the working Jews. In a letter to King Artaxerxes, the enemies of Judah convinced him to stall construction on the house of God.

My potential for abundant motherhood was limited when I explored jobs that would provide continuity to my salary and career success. But fellow Christians came alongside me and encouraged me to sacrificially follow God's plan.

Encouraged by God's Provision

> And God is able to bless you abundantly, so that in all things at all times, having all that you need, you will abound in every good work (2 Cor. 9:8 NIV).

The first promise that encouraged me to stop working was that God would provide financially for our family's reduced income.

How quickly God showed me I did not need to be a breadwinner anymore. For weeks our family collected unexpected checks in the mail like insurance refunds, investment returns, and overpaid medical bills. Further, my husband received several exciting promotions and bonuses at work.

I felt like the people of Judah departing my own exile with nothing to my name, completely dependent on others. When the Jews were leaving Babylon, they had no means to rebuild the temple. Yet God provided everything they needed by moving King Cyrus's heart. The king required the Babylonians to contribute silver, gold, livestock, and other goods as a freewill offering. Then the people of Judah took thousands of valuable articles up to the building site because of God's divine intervention.

God moved on others to provide for me and, to His credit, our income rose every month after I quit. I was awed by God's provision and inspired to bravely trust Him with our family finances.

Encouraged by God's Priority

> At that time, the disciples came to Jesus and asked, 'Who, then, is the greatest in the kingdom of heaven? He called a little child to him, and placed the child among them (Matt. 18:1-2 NIV).

When I felt torn about leaving the workforce, many former coworkers commended me for opting to be with my kids. They witnessed to me that prioritizing stay-at-home mom life for their own families helped them raise godly children.

Still, I struggled to turn down spiritual jobs like working in children's ministry at my church or becoming a missionary. God eventually convicted me that the church can survive without me, but my kids only grow up once.

Truly, as a Christian parent, I have the responsibility to impress God's commandments on my children all day long (Deut. 6:6-7). Although working can be good, quitting my formal job allowed me more time to intentionally disciple my children. Now I can spend time teaching them worship songs, reading them Bible stories, and serving in their church classes.

For the people of Judah, God held a different priority in mind when He freed them from exile in Babylon. Restoring the temple was the first step for proper Jewish customs like sacrifices and worship to resume. Further, God desired to dwell among His people within a magnificent temple. So, God spoke through King Cyrus to initiate the temple rebuilding as one of the first decrees during the king's reign.

God granted the people of Judah freedom for the initial purpose of temple reconstruction — other activities they missed during exile could wait. When I was given the chance to stop working, God led me to prioritize the nurture and spiritual growth of my children.

Encouraged by God's Peace

> The mind governed by the flesh is death, but the mind governed by the Spirit is life and peace (Rom. 8:6 NIV).

The final encouragement I needed came to me by the Holy Spirit. Each time I contemplated accepting one of the many job offers flooding in, I experienced unrest in my heart. I knew I had started on a path that would lead me outside of God's will by chasing money. Once I stopped that mad dash and began turning down those job offers, my soul found peace.

Fearful of earthly opposition, the people of Judah ignored God's instruction and allowed temple construction to stop for eighteen years. Then two prophets reminded the Jews to fear God's authority and some Jews commenced building again (Ezra 5:1).

Shortly after the people of Judah entered back into God's plan to rebuild the temple, God cleared up the conflict. King Darius found the original decree to support rebuilding the temple, adding that anyone who interfered would be overthrown (Ezra 6). The people of Judah were able to finish building in peace.

Once I focused on investing in my children, God resolved my internal conflict by making the job offers feel less urgent and giving me His peace.

Under God's Hand

> Because the hand of the Lord my God was on me, I took courage and gathered leaders from Israel to go up with me (Ezra 7:28 NIV).

Over the months following my start of stay-at-home motherhood, my confidence grew in God's provision, peace, and priority of family. One by one I courageously turned down jobs and the offers finally slowed down.

I no longer fear missing out on paychecks or work accolades, knowing that God's *righteous right hand* is strengthening, helping, and upholding me (Isa. 41:10 NIV). I can boldly yet politely decline job propositions by saying that I am exactly where God wants me.

By taking the opportunity to raise my daughters as a stay-at-home mom, my new "work" includes building up little temples of God. I am also solidifying my identity in Christ by giving up my identity as a careerwoman.

The people of Judah clearly lived under God's hand when they trusted Him to overcome opposition to rebuilding the temple. Praise flowed from their leader Ezra's lips of how the hand of God led, protected, and provided for the people of Judah. Sensing God's powerful presence gave the people of Judah the courage they needed to stay devoted to following and serving him.

I understand Ezra's praise because I have been encouraged by the gracious hand of God in my transition to full-time motherhood. When I took courage to abandon work completely, I enabled God to use me to raise children who know and love Him. God's people will never regret obeying His leading and trusting Him with their lives.

– 7 –
We Do Not Trust in Horses — or Mules
Anita Peluso

"We use mules instead of horses because they have a greater sense of self-preservation," remarked the guide. "Horses will run off a cliff if led to do so."

Trekking down the narrow North Kaibab Trail, our group considered the sure-footed mules as we gazed out over the steep ridges of the Grand Canyon. The guide instructed us to trust the instinct of the mules, relax, and enjoy the ride.

While I appreciated the instinctual self-preservation of my mule, I pondered how often people choose self-reliance over God's wisdom in difficult situations. Fear can cause us to react in a number of ways.

We may freeze where we are and make no move. We may run in the opposite direction as quickly as possible. Or, we may gather every sure-footed, reliable asset at our disposal—physical strength, money, knowledge—and muscle our way forward.

The courage of Joshua was put to the test as he led the Israelites into the land God promised to give them. The words God spoke to Joshua, *Be strong and courageous. Do not be afraid; do not be discouraged, for the Lord your God will be with you wherever you go*, read in Hebrew literally means to be strong physically, and in mind and heart (Josh. 1:9 ESV). Though God is encouraging Joshua to be strong, He is not telling him to buck up and rely on his own personal strength. Rather, God is calling Joshua to be strong in his commitment to God and to trust in *His* strength.

Moses gave the same charge to the Israelites on the shores of the Jordan before his death: Be strong and courageous. Do not fear or be in dread of them, for it is the Lord your God who goes with you. He will not leave you or forsake you (Deut. 31:6 ESV). Moses encouraged the Israelites to cross over into the land with their trust placed firmly in God's ability to enable them to take possession of it.

We learn from Joshua and Moses that courage requires both moving forward physically and the

We Do Not Trust in Horses—or Mules

mental confidence in God's wisdom and strength to accomplish what He has called us to do. James writes to the dispersed Israelites that faith must be accompanied with actions (James 2:14-26 ESV). Likewise, courage is shown by placing our trust in the Lord, then walking in the way He points us. Courage calls us away from our instinct of self-preservation and toward placing our full confidence in the Lord, who is strong, mighty, and wise.

The world encourages people to rely on their own abilities to overcome obstacles: enough money to buy what we need, enough knowledge to solve the problem, enough influence to change the situation. Contrary to the world, the Bible calls believers to regard physical attributes as of little value. Instead, we are to place our trust in the Lord our God. The psalmists declare the heart of courage as firmly trusting in God.

> Some trust in chariots and some in horses, but we trust in the name of the Lord our God. They collapse and fall but we rise and stand upright (Ps. 20:7-8 ESV).
>
> I will say to the Lord, my refuge and my fortress, my God, in whom I trust (Ps. 91:2 ESV).
>
> He is not afraid of bad news; his heart is firm, trusting in the Lord (Ps. 112:7 ESV).

When Jesus prepared the disciples for His impending death and resurrection, He encouraged them to take heart—have courage—so they would find peace in the difficult days ahead: *I have said these things to you, that in Me you may have peace. In the world you will have tribulation. But take heart: I have overcome the world* (John 16:33 ESV).

As we go through the trials and tribulations of life today, may we also find encouragement in His words to be strong and courageous, trusting in the Lord our God, not in ourselves, nor horses—or mules.

Take heart, dear friends. Our God is a mighty God!

– 8 –
The Minister's Daughter, Hard Exit
Elaine Juliusson

"So, this is where you went to college, Mom?" I brushed my son's hand and pointed toward Philadelphia Boulevard.

"I walked this street every day to get to class. Look! There's *The Rusty Monk*! I used to work there. There was a church somewhere close. The pastor and his wife were so kind to me one night when I was in trouble. I can't find it."

"Mom, you--in trouble? You were the strictest teacher at Arlington High! I was always getting flack about you from my friends! We have a plane to catch."

Elaine Juliusson

I turned the car toward I-605 South. But my mind brought me right back to Philadelphia Boulevard and Hadley Street. Nineteen years and it feels like yesterday.

* * *

The floorboards feel rough … cold beneath me. My head aches. I touch my face. Sticky. I should move.

Listen. Only my pounding heart. My jaw tightens, breathing stops. *Stay very still*. I hear the rhythmic sounds of deep snoring. Against pain I roll to my side. *Quiet, slow, push up*. My hands shake, knees quiver. *I must stand. I will stand.*

It was the same old fight, the same stale argument.

"I'm done, Rob."

"You won't go! You're mine! I own you."

"You treat me like … nothing!"

It was fast, his knuckles to my face. Twisting my arms, he forced me to the bed, his face close to mine, his breath putrid with alcohol and pot. I felt his flesh giving way under my nails. Moist. Slippery.

"You're nothing." I hit the floor. Discarded bone and flesh. "Don't move or I'll—"

Standing by the bed I watch him sleep. His face is soft, relaxed like a child. Like when we met. Now I know deception.

The Minister's Daughter, Hard Exit

I, too, can deceive! In darkness, my fingers find the car keys. I slip through the back door. A few steps, a turn of a key … I am free!

Exhilaration fades quickly. What was I thinking? Two hundred dollars in my purse, tip money I'd hidden from Rob. I grip the steering wheel. I should go back. He might be sleeping; he won't know …

A sharp horn pierces my ear, my body recoils. Awareness creeps in; I've been at a stop sign, I don't know how long. Black sky giving way to gray, I must move, decide. Stay. Go. I turn sharply onto a vaguely familiar street, not my usual path — school to home, home to school. A path walked in cold of winter, heat of summer. *You want a college education? Don't ask me for help. You're my wife. You don't' need it.*

A wife! How do I reconcile that? Isn't it a sin to break your vows with divorce? I'm supposed to stay for better or worse, in sickness and health, 'til death do us part. Will I lose my immortal soul if I leave? There is no love for God in Rob. He pushes me deeper and deeper into his sin. I think I will lose my immortal soul if I stay. I touch my stomach … swollen, tender. *What of you, if you are a "you?" Two months and waiting. Would you be the glue that holds us together, or a casualty?* A stab of pain. I must have been kicked.

"Jesus, if you can speak from Heaven, give me an answer!"

I parked, autopilot. Heaving sobs, waiting for an answer from God.

In the headlights I see a church. Lay all your burdens on Him. He will direct your path. Open 24 hours for prayer. My wicked voice groans. A little too convenient if you ask me. I've been hearing from my wicked voice too much lately. Don't act so smug. You're no Virgin Mary. Go back.

"No!" I scream loudly at my wicked voice.

My hand slips on the door handle before it opens. Letting the door slam behind me. I walk the path to church and push the door. Nothing. Shut solid. *Lies*, hisses my wicked voice. *Church lies!*

Angrily, I push with all my weight, falling into the sanctuary. Like in an altar call, I walk to the front and drop to my knees.

"Forgive me, Lord. I don't know what to do! If I stay, I sin. If I leave, I sin. I have prayed for direction, and nothing has changed. I must make a choice. Whatever happens, I choose you."

Forgiveness or retribution ... that's your choice.

Deep in prayer, I feel a touch on my shoulder. Terrified, I fall back on my heels to face my assailant.

"I'm so sorry. We didn't mean to frighten you. We

thought you heard us come in."

I slowly raise my eyes to a gentle, elderly face.

"Not too many take advantage of our prayer hours. I'm Pastor Jacobs. This is my wife, Mary." He extended his hand to help me to my feet.

"We saw the car and thought you might need help." Mary hugged me gingerly.

"Why would you think — ?"

"I suppose anyone coming to pray at this hour needs help." She smiled. "We heard your prayer."

"I left my husband." I felt foolish saying it.

"Ohhh." Mary shook her head sadly.

Here it comes. First compassion, then judgment. What are you thinking? That you'll get help? They'll tell you to go back, probably with a prayer.

Quiet, wicked voice! I don't want to hear from you!

You've seen plenty of false compassion, Preacher's Kid!

You're exaggerating, wicked voice!

"Mary, we should take our guest home for a cup of coffee. She could use one."

"Where are my manners! Of course, coffee! Would you like coffee, Miss …?"

"Kitty, my name is Kitty."

"Let's go, Kitty. Comfort awaits." Pastor Jacobs gave a sweeping courtly gesture toward the door, a playful smile on his face.

I walked between them toward the house. It was strange hearing my name. Other than at school I was "Hey, you" or "my old lady." Kitty … it was nice. Like I had a shred of humanity still in me. I stopped.

"My car. He'll see my car!"

"I can take care of that." Jacobs squeezed my shoulder. "I'll drive it into the garage. I'll meet you ladies in the house. You left the keys in the car."

"Stupid of me!"

"Don't be hard on yourself, Kitty."

"Come! Let's not delay," Mary hurried us. I'll never forget her kitchen — a warm cup of coffee, the sweet fragrance of cinnamon coffee cake — and her gentle hands.

"Well, now, I see you ladies attacked the cake without me!" Pastor Jacobs pulled a chair to the table. "The car's out of sight. Photo?" He looked at Mary as he handed her his cell phone.

"Photo? What–?" Fear covered me again.

"Kitty." Mary knelt by me. "Kitty, look." She touched my jeans, blood-stained. She held my hands, fingernails torn, my cheek bruised. "My dear child, we need to go to the hospital to treat your injuries. You'll need pictures to press charges."

"No hospital, no police. He'll get out of jail. It will be worse for me."

The Minister's Daughter, Hard Exit

"Where will you go? Do you have family?"

"My sister lives in Albuquerque. He won't chase me there, except for the car."

"Do you have gas money?" Pastor Jacobs joined in.

"Two hundred."

"Not enough." He shrugged. "Kitty, what you do is your decision. God doesn't want any of his children living in emotional or physical abuse. He will stay close to you whatever you do. There will be a ticket for Albuquerque at the United counter for you if you choose to use it. Be careful. We'll pray for your safety. Call us."

With thankfulness I hugged them. I needed one last deception.

I drove to the bus station, parked in long-term parking, then purchased a one-way ticket to Santa Cruz at the ticket counter. I purchased airport bus tokens at a different kiosk.

The Santa Cruz bus was boarding. A young couple were hugging good-bye.

"You're not going?"

"We don't have money for two tickets."

The girl added, "We have jobs in Santa Cruz. Our families are there."

I gave the boy my ticket, then barely made the bus to the airport. United Airlines had my ticket as promised. I boarded and settled in a window seat, ignoring the stares of passengers. My wounds would heal. My heart would heal. I turned my attention to the window and watched L.A. slip into the distance.

Thank you, Jesus. I'm free!

* * *

"You okay, Mom?"

"Sure. Why?"

"Looked like tears on your face."

"It's nothing." I brushed the wetness away. "An old memory."

"Mom, I'm choosing Albuquerque U. Let's call Dad!"

"Great college decision! When we board the plane, I'll tell you how dad and I met. It was a year after I moved to Albuquerque. You were one, running anywhere your chubby legs would take you, but that's our going home story and you'll have to wait."

Home, love, family. Thank you, Jesus, you set me free.

– 9 –

One Tiny Step
Terrie Hellard-Brown

One step

One tiny step

If I can just do it

But I'm frozen with fear

    Doubt

      Assumptions

      Imaginations

My heart beats with anxiety

Rather than life

One step

One tiny step

If I can just do it

Will the fear melt away

    And free me from this prison?

Will my pulse slow and quiet

    For me to hear Your Spirit?

Will I feel normal

    At least in that moment?

One step

One tiny step

If I can just do it

No one else may understand

That one step

One tiny step

    Is my Mount Everest

Taking it is

    Gold medal worthy

It gives me victory

    A real life

One step

One tiny step

I *can* just do it!

– 10 –
"With-You" Courage
Damon J. Gray

Even absent the ability to define courage, we know it when we see it, and we almost always admire it. A teenage boy hears, "It's cancer," and resolves to engage that battle. A woman loses her third child to miscarriage and determines to meet each sunrise with joy in her heart. A husband and father loses his job and engages whatever work he can find to support his family.

When the apostles Paul and Barnabas were in the city of Lystra, a city in central Anatole, Paul healed a man who had never walked. This healing was no private matter, having occurred as Paul was speaking before a sizable crowd. While doing so, Paul observed the crippled man and determined he had faith to be healed. Interrupting his address to the crowd, Paul spoke directly to the man, instructing him to stand upright on his feet and, to the amazement of the crowd, the man did so:

> And he sprang up and began walking. And when the crowds saw what Paul had done, they lifted up their voices, saying in Lycaonian, 'The gods have come down to us in the likeness of men!' (Acts 14:10b-11 ESV)

The people of Lystra erroneously concluded that gods had arrived, referring to Barnabas and Paul as Zeus and Hermes. To honor these gods, oxen and garlands were brought to the city gates with the intent of offering sacrifices to Barnabas and Paul. This, of course, was terribly distressing to the pair, but their circumstance was soon to degrade from merely distressing to decidedly perilous:

> But Jews came from Antioch and Iconium, and having persuaded the crowds, they stoned Paul and dragged him out of the city, supposing that he was dead (Acts 14:19 ESV).

With stunning capriciousness, the people of Lystra transitioned from wanting to sacrifice to Barnabas and Paul as gods to stoning Paul and unceremoniously dragging his lifeless body out of their city.

"With-You" Courage

Paul, who once watched with approval the stoning of Stephen, was now stoned himself. How quickly humanity moves from worshippers to executioners. How quickly the crowd crying, "Hosanna!" at the arrival of Jesus deteriorated into the same crowd crying, "Crucify! Crucify!" just days later.

Whether Paul was truly dead is a matter of ongoing debate, but what is clear is that he was sufficiently beaten and injured that the attacking crowd believed him to be dead. What happened next is a demonstration of courage that challenges our acceptance and comprehension:

> But when the disciples gathered about him, he rose up and entered the city, and on the next day he went on with Barnabas to Derbe (Acts 14:20 ESV).

When the fickle mobs of Lystra had just slain the keynote speaker at the day's event, it took great courage to go against the judgment of the riotous mob to align with that speaker. The new believers in Lystra gathered around the broken body of that man who had taught them about life in Christ, doubtless praying the best they knew how for guidance regarding what to do next. The danger was real, but they owned their newfound faith and honored the man by gathering round him, thus risking a stoning of their own. If Paul's healing of the lame man had amazed them, Paul rising from death or near death had to have been nothing short of astonishing. But what Paul did next demonstrated a level of courage that defied logic and common sense.

Having been beaten and left for dead, then rising from that beating, the logical course of action is to say, "Let's move on to the next city." Jesus instructed the disciples to wipe the dust from their feet against those cities that refused to welcome them or heed their words (Matt. 10:14). Paul and Barnabas arrived in Lystra because they were fleeing Iconium where there was a plot to stone them (Acts 14:5).

Having just been stoned in Lystra, not only did Paul return there with the believers, he visited the city twice more on subsequent missionary journeys. It is in Lystra that Paul later met and took on Timothy as his "son in the faith" (1 Tim. 1:2). And to further exemplify Paul's courage, on the return trip from Derbe, Paul and Barnabas stayed again not only in Lystra, but also Iconium, the city from which they initially fled, leading to their first visit to Lystra.

Individuals on a mission are not easily deterred, particularly when the God of Heaven has given that mission. Consider this call from Jesus on the life of Paul:

"With-You" Courage

> Now get up and stand on your feet. I have appeared to you to appoint you as a servant and as a witness of what you have seen of me and what I will show you. I will rescue you from your own people and from the Gentiles. I am sending you to open their eyes and turn them from darkness to light, and from the power of Satan to God, so that they may receive forgiveness of sins and a place among those who are sanctified by faith in me (Acts 26:16-18 NIV-1978).

Jesus gave Paul the calling, the purpose, and promised protection. With that triad of backing, any mission on which God sends us is a mission that can be engaged with an abundance of courage, and we embrace that mission, *striving side by side for the faith of the gospel, and not frightened in anything by your opponents. This is a clear sign to them of their destruction, but of your salvation, and that from God* (Phil. 1:27b-28 ESV).

Courage is rarely an attribute we generate within ourselves, out of our own stores of magnificence and valor. To believe otherwise is folly and demonstrates bravado unbecoming a disciple of Christ. Courage, rather, is most often spawned by an awareness of the one who's "got our back." One soldier has another soldier's back. Officers in law enforcement trust each other for support in time of need. Firefighters work in teams and safeguard one another. Inner-city gangs proliferate largely through that sense of belonging and the fact that members of the gang protect their own.

In the case of a disciple, our rearguard is no less than the God of the universe. With that reality in our pocket, we can walk courageously into any mission to which God calls us.

It has always been the case that God fights battles for his people. It was the case with David, with Jonathan, with Esther, with Gideon, with Moses, etc. Feel the strength of the call Yahweh gave to Zerubbabel and Joshua, and pay particular attention to the reason God offers for their courage:

> Yet now be strong, O Zerubbabel, declares the LORD. Be strong, O Joshua, son of Jehozadak, the high priest. Be strong, all you people of the land, declares the LORD. Work, for I am with you, declares the LORD of hosts (Acts 14:20 ESV).

Do not lose sight of that phrase, *for I am with you.* Yahweh is no less with us. He is arguably more so. Jesus said the Holy Spirit *dwells with you and will be in you* (John 14:17 ESV). That is a plane of "with you" that no Old Testament character knew.

We walk undaunted as sons and daughters of God. We walk boldly, not because of who we are, but because of who goes with us. With confidence and courage, we can align with David and say:

"With-You" Courage

The LORD is my rock and my fortress and my deliverer, my God, my rock, in whom I take refuge, my shield, and the horn of my salvation, my stronghold and my refuge, my savior; you save me from violence. I call upon the LORD, who is worthy to be praised, and I am saved from my enemies (2 Sam. 22:2 ESV).

– 11 –
Once More Unto the Breach
Christine Hagion

The morning light filtered through the kitchen window and the coffee pot gurgled as I grabbed a mug. My girls weren't awake yet and, in the stillness, I felt alone.

After leaving my abusive husband, I'd prayed a brave, resolute prayer: "Lord, I'm terrible at picking men. If I'm ever to remarry, Father, You must choose him." In the years since, friends and family members tried to set me up with men they viewed as potential partners, but I'd declined them all. "Thank you, no," I'd say, shaking my head gently. "I'm not interested in dating at this time." Instead, I funneled my efforts into parenting my two daughters on my own, all while working and attending college.

But now, I finally felt ready for a relationship. *Father, it's been ten years already. Where is he?* I waited a moment for His response, staring at a poster on my kitchen cabinet that said: "I don't know all the answers. But I know the One who does." Then I heard God's answer deep within my heart.

Well, you might be ready right now, but he's not.

Okay, God! Sounds like You've got this all figured out. I'll wait and trust Your perfect timing. I felt His perfect peace.

* * *

A few years after that impatient prayer in my kitchen, YoHan, whom I'd just met at the gym, sat with me in the frothy bubbles of the jacuzzi. YoHan offered to set me up with someone at the software firm where they worked. He prattled on about how his boss had recently divorced, quit smoking, and lost a bunch of weight.

Great. Sounds like a loser. No thank you. I was prepared with my knee-jerk response.

Wait. Not so fast, the Holy Spirit chided me.

What? Did I hear this right?

Hear him out, the Holy Spirit prompted.

I guess this must be a ministry opportunity. I'll see what I can do to help, I mused.

"Although he's divorced, he still meets with his ex every weekend for breakfast with the kids," YoHan boasted.

Hmmm. My interest was piqued. *This sounds like an unusual scenario. Perhaps it might be worth pursuing.*

"Okay, I'll meet with him. For coffee," I conceded, looking for a low-risk setting. "But only if you join us. I won't see him alone." Because of my experiences with my ex-husband, safety issues were ever-present in my mind. "Don't get your hopes up, though," I cautioned. "I have lots of room in my life for friends, but not dating." YoHan agreed.

A week later, the three of us met at Orchard Valley Coffee and sipped our espressos, sitting outside on wrought iron chairs. YoHan introduced Vic, a middle-aged man with a tan and dark hair graying at the temples. He appeared impressed with my community involvement and interest in performing arts.

"So, you're a thespian, huh?" Vic asked.

"I was. Years ago." I didn't reveal that I'd needed to abandon my dreams of acting, change my name, have reconstructive surgery on my face, and relocate hundreds of miles away so my abuser wouldn't be able to find me. A cool breeze ruffled my dress. I looked down, smoothing out the fabric over my knee.

Vic informed me that he and Yohan lifted weights daily at lunchtime.

"Yeah," YoHan said. "He just won a weightlifting competition. A dead lift of 850 pounds!" With Vic's newfound love of fitness after his divorce, and my new career, it seemed we were both on the path of rediscovering ourselves.

"Hey, we should all work out together!" YoHan suggested.

* * *

In the following weeks, YoHan, Vic, and I met several times at the gym. One day, after our workout, Vic walked with me out to my car.

"Want to grab coffee?" he asked casually.

"Sure," I agreed, assuming there was nothing more to this than a blossoming friendship. We drove together in his red Mustang and, when we arrived, an alarming thought ensnared me. *Oh no! I put myself into a situation where I could be compromised. I never do that!* I shuddered for a moment, fear overtaking me. *Would I be victimized again, as before?* I centered myself, checking in with the Holy Spirit.

You have nothing to fear, He said. The response calmed my mind. Vic opened my passenger door.

"I guess chivalry is not dead," I quipped.

"Indubitably," Vic replied.

That day, we talked for hours about his prior service as a Navy SEAL who'd served in Vietnam. *Indeed, there is more to this guy after all!*

Vic treated me and both my children to second-row center seats at the *Phantom of the Opera* in San Francisco. The first time we met alone—just the two of us—for dinner, I realized how comfortable I felt in Vic's presence, and the absence of danger was a welcome difference from my last foray into romance. I appreciated his slow manner of courtship, without pressure. Exactly how much, I'm sure he didn't know. He waited three weeks to kiss me.

One night, we went dancing, and Vic bought me a dozen red roses. I inhaled their soft fragrance, and the Holy Spirit interrupted my reverie.

He's the one.

What? My mind reeled. *I couldn't have heard right.* But I recognized the Divine Voice as He spoke to my spirit. The music swelled and Vic stretched out his hand, inviting me back onto the dance floor. Vic spun me, and I twirled to the rhythmic beat of the band.

After returning home, while brushing my teeth, I asked, *Lord, what's this about Vic being 'the one?'* Suddenly, I recalled the vow I'd made to not seek a companion. The Lord had chosen, as requested.

* * *

About a month later, Vic and I drove along the beachside highway in Monterey in his convertible, stopping at the iconic cypress tree on a rocky cliff overlooking the Pacific Ocean. We climbed out and took in the breathtaking view, hearing waves crashing below. On our way back to the car, I teetered on a rock, and Vic kneeled, extending his hand—I thought—to help stabilize me.

"Would you do me the honor of becoming my bride?" Vic asked.

I would've been taken aback at his proposal if the Holy Spirit hadn't spoken to me about it beforehand. The gulls cried, and another wave sprayed us with salty ocean water. I accepted, delirious from emotion and the gorgeous scenery.

That night, at Vic's home, he poured me a glass of Chardonnay and turned on his stereo, playing the classic song by Blood, Sweat, and Tears. "You've made me so very happy," Vic sang aloud to the music as he sat down next to me on the couch. "I'm so glad you came into my life," he serenaded me while holding my hand.

How romantic! And he has a wonderful singing voice! I was blissful in the moment, but later, fear began to creep in.

Back at home, while I should've begun planning my wedding, doubts arose. *Could I trust him?* I'd only known him a few months. *And what about my kids? Will they accept him? What kind of a father figure might he be? Will it be safe for them?* Again, the Lord reminded me I'd given Him the prerogative over whether I was to marry again and whom my groom would be.

I recalled the verses I'd recited to myself all those years before when I'd feared my abuser would find me and finish me off, as he'd promised. They'd helped me overcome the dread that encroached upon me after fleeing my nightmare of a marriage.

Be strong and courageous, the Scripture said, resounding in my mind as though it were spoken aloud. *As I was with Moses, so I will be with you; I will never leave you nor forsake you. Do not be afraid; do not be discouraged, for the* LORD *your God will be with you wherever you go* (Josh. 1:5, 9 NIV).

God's Word reverberated in my soul. I crouched down on the carpet beside my bed, bowing my back despite the pain in doing so, having been injured by my batterer. I clasped my hands in surrender, crying aloud in desperation.

"Okay, Lord. I don't know if I can trust Vic. But I do know that I can trust You. And since You chose him for me, I will obey."

* * *

About a year later, I walked down the aisle in my champagne dress with lace and pearls, my veil blowing in the wind. A line from Shakespeare's classic play, *Henry V*, replayed in my mind. "Once more unto the breach," King Henry had called, to rally his men before attacking the French.

I remembered the battleground of my first marriage all too well. Reentering marriage was daunting. But now, cheered on by the Holy Spirit, my constant companion, I knew I would emerge victorious in this divinely arranged union.

Vic and I will celebrate our twenty-fifth anniversary this summer.

– 12 –

Learning Courage
Heather Popish

I used to think

courage is a trait we're born with.

Something out of reach

of my fearful nature.

But I have learned

that courage is gradually built up.

Moment by moment,

and experience by experience.

Heather Popish

I watch my little one
learn this each day.
To try and fail, then
get back up and smile again.

My sweet child
learning at such a young age
that with God
all things are possible.

You don't give up,
though you might cry.
You have courage
and again you try.

Thank You, God,
for sending my little child
to teach me that it's never too late
to learn to be courageous.

> *For the Spirit God gave us does not make us timid, but gives us power, love, and self-discipline (2 Tim. 1:7 NIV).*

– 13 –
The Bravest Girl
Robynne Elizabeth Miller

The gym's viewing box was crowded with other moms, most of whom seemed to know each other well. They laughed, chatted, and set up play dates in the minutes before the day's gymnastic showcase began, exchanging tips for beating the Sacramento Valley summer heat and the best ways to combat vacation boredom.

I knew no one, despite sitting with most of these people every week for the past three months. This was partially due to my inherent shyness, which was painfully ever-present in social situations. But there also hadn't been time to venture a "hello" to anyone before the pre-school class began.

Each week, I'd arrive at the gym early, my four-year-old daughter clinging to my hand and pressing herself into my side. We'd enter the viewing box and head to the upper left corner. I'd sit and pat the seat next to me, but every single week she'd climb into my lap, eyes wide and brimming with tears, instead.

The gym was large, with several classes and practices always in session, and the noise needed some acclimating to by my sensory-challenged girl. So, with arms wrapped tightly around her, I'd gently rock and, with a low voice, begin to speak.

"Look at that girl in the blue shirt ... she's learning how to vault over that bar ... And isn't that boy flexible? He's doing the splits! ... see the girl by the woman with the whistle around her neck? Aren't her curls lovely? ..."

When I felt her heartbeat and breathing slow, and her tense body begin to relax, I'd continue, changing my focus to get her ready.

"Isn't that the pit you get to jump into? It was so fun when you landed in all that foam ... and that big trampoline looks so bouncy! You had a beautiful smile when you jumped on it with your friends! ... Which is the mat you learned to do a somersault on? The small one near the trampoline, or the big one in front of us?"

Slowly, whispered answers would begin to slip from her lips. "The pit was fun ... I learned to somersault on the big mat."

By the time the viewing box began to fill, and her classmates started gathering on the floor, she was usually ready to join them. Today, however, she was more hesitant than usual.

"Will you stay here, Mama?" she asked, as she had every single week.

"Yes, baby girl. I'll be right here. This is your last class and I have to take video so Papa and Grandma and Grandpa can see what you can do."

I kissed the top of her head and then, looking into her eyes, said, "It's time for class to start. I promise I'll be here the whole time."

She managed a small smile, then looked at the jostling, giggling children grouped near her teacher just a few yards away. The smile disappeared, and her body tensed again.

I leaned down close to her ear. "You can do this, brave girl. You've been doing great every class, and I know you can do this, too."

Her hazel eyes, framed by impossibly long eyelashes, looked up at me. She wasn't convinced, but nodded anyway. Slipping through the opening at the front of the viewing box, she slowly walked toward her class.

The crowd was larger than usual, with dads and a few grandparents coming to view the last-class showcase. Not a seat was empty as the teacher began her end-of-term speech.

I heard none of it.

My eyes were locked on my little olive-skinned girl, sitting at the back of the group, her wide eyes filled with fear.

I first met her when she was two, though she'd entered the foster care system as a baby. The reunification process hadn't gone well, so her social workers decided to change placements. Our county matched children who might become available for adoption with families willing to support the reunification process and simultaneously commit to permanency if that became an option. It was called "high-risk adoption," and it was aptly named. While better in every way for the child, it presented enormous emotional risks to potential parents.

We loved her through a year-and-a-half of court hearings, visits with bio mom, and endless therapies and meetings before a judge decided that all resources and options had been exhausted, and it was time for a permanent home.

Our love for her hadn't started the day she was freed for adoption, though, nor the year later when she became legally ours. It started the first moment we laid eyes on her curly hair and deep-set dimples. Instantly, a deep, fierce, and profound sense of maternal love enveloped me. Whether she stayed for a season or forever, I loved her with all my heart.

She was a ball of fear in those first days ... terrified of men, playpens, stairs, and being hungry. Her body, drug addicted at birth, shook violently upon every waking. We kept her away from playpens and steps, made sure she always had access to food, and let her dictate the pace of connection with my husband.

Every morning, and after every nap, I'd hold her trembling body close, rocking, praying, and speaking life into her until she finally stilled. As her little body healed, her heart began to, as well. She started learning to trust, and slowly overcame her fears.

Movement on the mat brought my wandering thoughts back to the moment. The teacher's speech ended, and the children lined up to demonstrate their gymnastics skills. They rolled and somersaulted, bounced and jumped in the air. As a big finish, the teacher announced, the children would crawl along three balance beams: the first one low to the ground, and the next two progressively higher. It was supposed to demonstrate balance and strength.

My stomach clenched. The look of terror on my daughter's face, and the way she stood frozen, said it all. The children had never attempted this skill using beams off the ground.

Somehow, my sweet girl ended up in the middle of the line and, when instructed, began crawling along the first beam. She moved slowly, but steadily, along its length. By the time she came to the transition up to the next beam, a small gap had opened between her and those before her.

Lips pressed into a thin line, she carefully climbed to the next section. Once that transition was safely navigated, she paused, eyes locked on the beam beneath her, before inching forward. Her tiny hands gripped tightly, color draining from her fingers. Small beads of sweat glistened on her forehead and, by the time she was halfway across the second beam, those ahead of her had already dismounted the third.

That's when I became aware of voices around me.

She's holding up the line ... she's obviously too afraid to finish ... we'll be here all day! ... why don't they pull her off and let the competent kids through?

Suddenly, I didn't feel very introverted.

"Please be quiet," I heard myself saying. "My daughter doesn't need to hear your comments."

The Bravest Girl

The murmuring lapsed into an uncomfortable silence until someone said, "Why don't you go get her? She's obviously too scared and she's holding up those who actually have some ability."

I looked at the woman, willing myself to keep my voice steady and respectful.

"What is your child afraid of?" I asked.

"Afraid of?" she replied, clearly puzzled.

"Yes. What is she afraid of?"

The lady rolled her eyes and crossed her arms. "Well … large dogs and fireworks, I guess. What does that have to do with …"

"When is the last time she approached a large dog?" I asked. "Or held a sparkler?"

"She wouldn't do those things," the woman snapped. "I just told you … she's afraid."

"Exactly," I replied. "And *my* girl is terrified of heights. My adopted-from-the-foster-care-system daughter, whose first two years were filled with more trauma, abuse, and neglect than most people experience in a lifetime, is *terrified* of heights. But she's up there. Maybe she's slower than your unafraid children. *But my daughter's up there.*"

The woman's mouth opened, then shut. She looked at me, then toward my girl, who was navigating the last turn onto the highest beam. I turned, too, my eyes burning with hot tears.

After a few silent moments, a man called out, then others joined in. Soon the whole viewing box was filled with shouts of encouragement.

Keep going! You can do it! Brave girl! You're doing great! Almost there!

When the class was dismissed, many people crowded around my daughter, offering high fives and congratulations. It was several minutes before she squeezed through and ran into my waiting arms, flushed and a little shaky, but beaming.

"Did you see me, Mama?"

I wrapped her up in a huge hug and whispered into her ear, "Yes, my brave, brave girl. I sure did."

– 14 –
Finding Courage
D.H. Weinberg

A firefighter. A policeman. Someone in the military. Many would say they're the definition of courage. Perhaps. Some may also say they're just performing a job they signed up for and have been trained to do. Also, perhaps.

If you're a believer, David versus Goliath, Joshua versus Jericho, or Moses versus the Egyptians might come to mind. Yes, those three were courageous. However, we have a very narrow definition of courage sometimes, and often miss many who exemplify courage regularly, or even every day.

D.H. Weinberg

Courage has often been defined as "not the absence of fear, but doing the thing you fear anyway." It's doing something that is risky, dangerous, or comes at a cost. Most people today would describe the actions of President Zelensky, the President of Ukraine, as the epitome of courage. Risky, dangerous, and coming at a cost? Check, check, and check.

However, courage isn't just about great heroics ... saving lives ... vanquishing a foe. It's not just David versus Goliath, or Zelensky versus Putin. Often, there are no publicized heroics with acts of courage. For instance:

- The teacher or student who endures ridicule and scorn because they stand up for their beliefs and unpopular principles.
- The politician who risks losing office because they vote their conscience, rather than do what's politically expedient to get themselves re-elected.
- The worker who risks losing their job or being side-lined because they stand up against sexual harassment, racism, corruption, or various kinds of injustice.
- The person who's been wronged, yet forgives — and leaves vengeance to God.

- The speaker, author, or faith-follower who articulates their beliefs and worldview, knowing they'll receive criticism, condemnation, and sometimes shaming and shunning, even by close friends, family members, or other faith followers.
- The believer who risks prison, torture, or death in a foreign country that doesn't tolerate Christianity.

And then there was Jesus, who had both the courage and love to go to the cross for all of us. Despite being wronged. Despite the cost. Despite what He knew was coming. Betrayal. Hatred. False Accusations. Torture. Death. How many of us would endure this ending, if we knew what was ahead?

Plus, it wasn't just in death that Jesus showed courage and love. He touched lepers. He sought out the demon-possessed. He had dinners with tax collectors and the outcasts of society. He said things He knew would make some of the religious leaders incensed enough to kill Him, and make some of His devoted followers leave. He counted the cost, but did these things anyway. Risky, dangerous, and comes at a cost? Check, check, and check.

But, let's face it. Some people are just more courageous by nature, while most of us struggle with fear and courage. Sadly, God doesn't take our nature and nurture as an excuse. One only needs to look at the twelve disciples Jesus called to see that. No! God recognizes our humanity, but calls everybody to have courage. The words, *Fear not!* permeate the Scriptures. The Apostle Paul also says in Philippians 4:13 (NASB), *I can do all things through Him who strengthens me.* That includes being courageous.

So, how does one become courageous? I believe the key words in Philippians 4:13 are *through Him.* Through Jesus. Neither Paul nor Jesus expects us to do all things, or tough things, in our own strength and courage. We all know Isaiah 40:31 (NASB), *Yet those who wait for the Lord will gain new strength.* Are we really relying on God to provide strength and courage, or are we secretly believing we can do miraculous things, beyond our capabilities, with the courage and strength we possess?

So often I've found that God lets me flail away in my own strength or run away due to fear and lack of courage. Then, it's almost like I hear him saying *Are you done now? Are you ready to give it all to me?* I've discovered that it's only when I finally yield to Him that He gives me the courage to face and fight the really hard stuff in life.

For the believer, isn't one definition of courage just that: giving our problems to God and relying on Him and not ourselves? Isn't surrendering to God, whether in big or small things, the ultimate act of courage? It takes courage and faith to hand over the big things to God and just let go. To say, "Thy will, not mine, be done." To say, "Yes, Lord" — even when we're terrified.

Isn't surrendering to God what Joshua did when he attacked Jericho, the impregnable city? What Moses did by standing up to Pharoah? What David did? Hezekiah did? What Rehab, Ruth, and Mary did? What the disciples did when they left everything and followed Jesus? What the Apostle Stephen did when he defied the Jewish authorities? What the disciples did when they were put into prison and instructed not to preach Jesus, and Peter said courageously: *We must obey God rather than men*? (Acts 5:29 NASB)

Did any of these people act courageously in their own strength? No! They said *Yes* to God, and He provided courage at the moment they needed it. We can do some courageous things on our own, depending on our personality and experience. However, courage to do the really big and hard things that God requires of most of us only comes from the Lord.

It also comes from experience and usually over time. So often we compare ourselves to Biblical figures or others we admire and wonder *Why can't I be like that?* We don't realize (or we forget) that courage is typically built experience by experience, and a little bit at a time. Just like our faith. Seeing God come through helps us believe He'll come through for us again the next time. The disciples could only spread the Gospel by seeing, hearing, and observing Jesus in person, daily, and for three years! It took Moses forty years in the wilderness before he was ready and equipped to be God's leader of the Israelites.

Therefore, if you want to be more courageous, start with the little things in your life. Start with the things that are on your plate right now. How can you be courageous in what you're dealing with now? How can you surrender it to God? Have you said "Thy will, not mine be done?"

What's one thing you've run away from or procrastinated on or been afraid of doing that you know you need to overcome? Start small. Give it to God, and ask for His help and the courage to face it. Get a little bit more courageous today in something. Tackle something you've been afraid of trying—in partnership with the Almighty.

Finding Courage

Firefighters who run into burning buildings didn't do that at the start. Police who go in after an armed robber were trained to face that very situation. Soldiers who go into battle were trained to fight and, over time, they gained the experience and confidence to go back into battle the next day.

Courage is built little by little. As our faith grows in God's goodness and from each experience of His faithfulness, so our courage will grow likewise. Therefore …

What small thing can you do today, right now, to be a little more courageous?

– 15 –
Terror and the Paper Bags
Karen D. Wood

The cold metal tables were immovable, anchored to the cement floor of the cinder block room. Twice a week, through endless seasons, parents came to those tables to meet their children.

Two hours allowed time to visit. Terror was their constant companion as they were physically searched and then escorted deep into the heart of the juvenile hall, past bars and slamming metal doors that shut them in, to the tables.

She arrived with her husband again. How could she be expected to sit still and not desperately cling to her sixteen-year-old? She'd wring her hands as she battled the panic at the growing seriousness of the case keeping her son behind bars.

Would he be simply staring, cold and blank? Would his face be twisted with rage over another unpleasant encounter in custody?

He settled lightly into the bench facing them, tense as a snake coiled to strike. The three of them were together. Dad reached into his shirt pocket with steady hands and held a 3 x 5 card of topic notes to try to carry the conversation. Their son never fully relaxed, constantly assessing every sight and sound in the room.

Making several trips to a water cooler across the room, she filled up little paper cups for him. He was so thirsty.

After he passed her each empty cup, she fidgeted with it as she kept her hands carefully in the open on the table's still-cold surface. As she crumpled the fragile cup, she could hear the wax coating separate from the paper, dropping a small flurry of bits onto the metal. She tore the cup apart at its seam, making a small, flat curve. She tore out a heart shape, and then added more shapes. Heart, spade, diamond, club. Each linked to the next. Her son followed with his eyes as she pushed the finished chain across the table. He held the shapes and tried to smile, but they both

Terror and the Paper Bags

knew he couldn't keep it. That would require being approved by the guards, ever watching from the corners. Just glancing at them made her cringe and shrink. *Were they the ones that allowed her son to be beaten up after the completely unexpected arrest?*

When the time was up, she held the bits of torn paper during the brief goodbye hug they were allowed.

Leaving him there and returning home, she held the wax paper chain in her hands, sobbing through many nights.

Late one night, a call came that her son had been beaten up. Again. She clutched the torn paper as she tried to fall back into a restless sleep, wishing she could touch him, comfort him.

The next visit, they returned to the tables and were told snacks could be purchased. Dad brought back a full paper bag. She felt some joy in getting to see their son eat something. Soon an empty bag was on the table. She started smoothing it out, folding and refolding. Fingers fidgeting. As before, she found the seams and opened the bag, laying it flat. It became 11 x 21 inches of distraction, something to help visitation time pass.

She started thinking about ripping out a turtle for him, knowing how much he loved them. *How to make it fit within that rectangular shape?* Soon the head appeared, peeking out of the shell. Her son was curious to see what was happening. *Hmm, how could she make the scute shapes of the outside of the shell?* She ripped very thin strips for the outlines, so the shapes would not fall out. As she tore out the feet, she saw a few more smiles as he recognized what it was becoming. A carefully torn tail finished another sculpture, and the visit was over.

Leaving wasn't getting any easier. She often had to stop and hang onto the cold bars in the hallway for a few minutes before being able to exit the building. She was leaving her boy behind, and all her strength had been spent holding back so many unanswered questions. *How could it be that her boy was in this place? How will it end?* Somehow, she felt a strange comfort in guarding his turtle.

Week followed week, meeting at the table. Terror was still her constant companion during those visits. *Would yet another kid be taken to the ground in the middle of the visit, dragged to another room, with so much yelling and screaming?* The sounds just echoed. Leaving after that visit, she had glanced back to see blood being hosed off the floor in that next room.

Each week, she quietly hoped another paper bag would be on the table. During the week she found herself wondering what could be ripped into the bag,

Terror and the Paper Bags

anything to distract both her and her son from the terrors — to amuse, to bring some encouragement into the visit.

She tore out a few letters, attached to her own favorite: a giraffe with the spots carefully torn away. YKHMILY. Code for "You Know How Much I Love You," which brought big smiles. Another week, a few more words were added. Then whole sentences. "Trust in the Lord with all your heart and lean not on your own understanding," which was his favorite Bible verse.

Ripping out so many words was a game of positive and negative space, connecting letters and shapes. Tiny connecting bridges were made, so the counters (the middles of the letters), wouldn't fall out. Letters like A, B, D, and O all took special care. Some weeks the letters were formed in calligraphy, as if a quill pen were removing the paper. Trying to use the whole canvas of the paper bag without it falling apart became part of the distraction, so many words and images ripped into it that the paper started looking like lace.

The constant sound of gentle tearing became a soothing sound for all of them at the cold table, soon covered with piles of leftover bits. Soon, other kids and families started watching, wondering and waiting to see the finished product. They weren't supposed to talk between tables, but the finished bag held up and passed around broke the barriers.

The paper became pictorial: A door opened on a large hand holding a globe and key, to remind him who held the key to his life, and it wasn't the guards.

But even the guards would come to see the visit's summary in paper. Those dreaded guards, who were gradually turning into humans. She even found herself talking to them—at least a few of them—expressing gratitude for their care for her son.

One guard approved her son keeping the torn bags. He stowed the collection under his mattress. Her son's cellmates, so young like him, would ask to look at them when they were upset. It gave them something to take their minds off their situations, something to anticipate as their trials came and went, as they made friends and then had to leave each other. Touching the ripped paper calmed them down.

Her son's trial loomed, and the hands tearing the paper were often shaky. Her birthday arrived. Then his. The seasons and holidays came and went, each with new layers of distress. A Christmas tree appeared out of one bag, with presents of paper packages, as no other gifts could be given this year.

By the end of the visits, all four seasons had passed. She wondered how to represent the concept of so

Terror and the Paper Bags

many seemingly lost days. She made a large square, started at the middle, and ripped out four trees, each extending to the corners of the bag. One full tree. Another with leaves falling. Another bare. A fourth with a few new leaves. Each tree connected by the words summer, springtime, winter, and harvest. In the middle the roots became "Great is Thy Faithfulness." She hummed the old hymn while she ripped small shapes that looked like they had been cut by scissors. More paper lace. More gratitude for lessons learned and the year about to be over. This art piece was added to the dozens and dozens created in the visits at the cold table.

One of the last brown paper bag creations had a large hand holding a fishing pole made from a paper cup. From another cup, she made a ball of fishing line. As she looked at it, she smiled wistfully and held it up to him. He saw it and returned an echo of her smile. Without planning, the ball looked like a turtle. She couldn't wait to take her boy fishing at the lake.

The year of visits ended, and the couple cautiously drove their boy and all the bags home, knowing it was only the beginning of an even longer road. Yet she was stronger, with a soul acquainted with terror, finding courage tearing paper bags.

– 16 –
Courage, COVID, and Standing Up for Christ
Carlitta Cole-Kelly

In the background I could hear my sister, Faren, wailing loudly on my cell phone. Her daughter, Lajuante (pronounced La-wan-tee), had just died of what she thought was a severe case of influenza. Our family in Mississippi was grief-stricken and knew we needed to make funeral arrangements soon. Cause of death? Unknown.

My mother tried earnestly to paint a picture of what later transpired at the funeral home while planning Lajuante's services.

"I nearly fell off my seat when she said it!" my mother exclaimed, while recalling her conversation with the funeral home director.

"Who was she talking about?" I pressed, trying to clarify the details and who was at the mortuary. Mom had asked a simple question among the three participants.

"So, who's going to do Lajuante's make-up and hair?" my mother had asked the funeral home director. The director had looked across the desk, first at my mother, then toward Faren.

Without hesitation, the director replied, "Faren always does a good job with our clients."

"What? What are you talking about?" I squealed on the phone at my mother, stunned.

Our family had neglected to consider my youngest sister's talents, skills, and ingenuity which encapsulated just part of who she was. In happier days, her uplifting laughter and social acumen had brightened many settings.

"What y'all got going on up in here?" Faren's voice would boom across a room, followed by boisterous laughter—the kind that permeated any uncomfortable atmosphere. In years past, she and her husband, Yul, Lajuante's father, were often comedic winners at the Bid Whist table. After beating worthy opponents, the two would stand and do their Super Mario Brothers rubbing belly dance celebration as laughter peeled across the room.

Most of all, Faren liked extolling that she had two college graduate children and tried to love all four of her children the best way she knew. She also kept them looking good. In her twenties, Faren had become a licensed cosmetologist, giving family and friends big discounts whenever she could.

However, all of that happened years before the fall, long before enemies, known and unknown, would wreak havoc in Faren's life. It was before addiction became a stronghold, as it continues to be for thousands of others today. However, despite the addiction, she still made women and men look stylish and beautiful, even if she could no longer weave together that same essence for herself.

"Mom, she can't do that!" I'd protested, then acquiesced, "Can she?"

"Apparently so," my mother replied. No one in the family had known about this side job of Faren's at the funeral home—that of doing hair and make-up of the deceased.

During the days leading up to Lajuante's funeral, I'd tried, but failed, to find words to comfort my sister, who, at age forty-eight, had now lost her only daughter. She was a single mom, had made the Dean's List in college, graduated, and had been the top sales producer at her job. She stayed home from work one day to fight symptoms that, just two months later, would shut down the United States. Those symptoms evolved into what we now know as COVID-19.

No autopsy was done for Lajuante.

My son, daughter-in-law, and I flew maskless into New Orleans, then drove into Mississippi to attend the service.

"She's going to do what?" I balked upon hearing what Faren had planned next, as if the hair and the make-up task weren't enough. On the day of the funeral, I stood outside the church, creeping further along in the funeral procession line—late again. My sister had positioned herself at the bottom of the church steps near a concrete stoop facing the line of mourners. Stockingless, wearing white pumps and a pink lace dress with quarter-length sleeves, Faren had on black-rimmed eyeglasses and a short dark wig. She even looked stoic as she greeted the sad faces that approached her. A rare smile revealed her still perfect white teeth.

I searched her face for anything unfamiliar, worried about how she would hold up. On the day of the funeral, however, I saw no reddened eyes, no tears, no slurred speech, and no appearance of being high or otherwise incapacitated. The few words she spoke gave no hint of anger, confusion, or any of the other disruptive behaviors I'd been warned my sister could display while enduring her disease.

At the final viewing before the funeral, I glanced through watery eyes at my niece in the coffin. Her hands were folded neatly in place, her even-toned brown skin glistened with a smooth, soft innocence, and her hair flowed down well past her shoulders in long swirls of braided curls. Her make-up was flawless and beautifully done: lipstick, black mascara, liner, and pale lavender eye shadow to match the elegant white and lavender dress that resembled a choir robe at the front. She was a daughter of the King, well-prepared and en route to meet her Master.

That was the one assurance in such overwhelming sadness and gloom that, despite everything, we all, including my son, niece, sisters, and brother, had grown up in the church. Though imperfect, we had accepted Christ as our personal Savior at some point in our lives, been baptized, and fully expected to meet up with loved ones again someday. But there was still one more challenge left here in the present.

I sat stiffly on the cushioned church bench with my knees pressed together, clenching my hands and looking down, uncertain of what would come next. Some of Lajuante's close friends and cousins had already started to wail loudly. Then, overcome with emotion, they left the church early to go outside.

Striding up to the front at the appointed time walked Faren, taking her place at the microphone. We held our breath. Then, that booming, spirited voice that in years past had blended with many choirs, blessed pews of parishioners, caused some to shout in their seats and others to raise out of theirs, was back! Her singing, another gift, was as inspiring and uplifting as when she first soloed the song, *Stand Up for Christ,* on a concert stage in California. That powerful, personified mix of soprano and alto was once again singing praises to the Lord, only this time at the funeral of her own daughter. I could not believe what I was hearing or witnessing. Only once did her voice crack with emotion, but with the child of God's consummate talent, she did not let it deter her. She regrouped in seconds and finished just like before. Afterward, Faren walked back to her seat unattended, as calmly as she'd come.

"Sister Faren, I didn't know you could sang like that!" exclaimed the Pastor. "You gonna have to come on back to church and bless us with that voice of yours," he added, preparing to give the eulogy.

Months later, Faren left a voice message on my phone thanking me for helping her replace her ID and obtain a cell phone; she was hoping to get her life back on track. I kept the message and still play it from time to time, as I do the videos we have. How she ever had the courage to do her deceased daughter's make-up and hair and sing at her funeral will forever astound and amaze me, but not God's grace.

It was grace that held our family together when we also lost Faren to a second brain aneurysm just eight months after her daughter died. My mother had thanked God at the time that it wasn't an overdose in a dark, drug-infested alley somewhere that consumed her. Even Faren's partner shared that he sometimes heard her praying, asking God to deliver her from her addiction.

Yes, it was God's grace and mercy that helped us get through Lajuante's passing at age thirty, through Faren's death at age forty-eight, and through the death of my beloved brother who, at age forty-four, succumbed to COVID 19 just one month after attending Faren's funeral.

It is this same portion of grace and mercy that sustains us … that roots and grounds our belief in the promises of God … that assures us no weapon formed against any of us shall ever succeed … that reminds us that His mercies are renewed every single morning. It is the same God whom we can thank for allowing us to witness Faren's courage and determination and what it takes to "Stand Up for Christ," regardless of devastating situations. Finally, it is God's eternal love that ensures we have the courage, strength, and determination, even during our grief, to make it through.

– 17 –
Adventure is on the Other Side of Fear
Darcy Schock

I clenched my fists, nails biting into my palms. If I gripped harder, maybe this wouldn't slip through my fingers. I didn't want to be here, standing in the kitchen, face-to-face with my husband. Something resembling words came out of his mouth. My thoughts screamed louder than his voice. *I can't let go, not even a little.*

He stared at me, expecting a response.

"What did you say?" I forced myself to focus on the words coming from his lips this time.

"You're hurting your family in this pursuit," he repeated.

The truth vocalized landed heavy on my heart and burned through my chest. My husband finally said what I knew, but refused to face. I bit my tongue, refraining from listing all the reasons I couldn't back off. Deep down, I knew they were only attempts to hide the festering wound of trying to find value in my work.

The darkness I had avoided for so long rose, staring me in the face. What started as good intentions had morphed into something much different. I could no longer be in control. Change needed to happen, but that scared the living daylights out of me.

Over the next couple of days, the Spirit worked in my heart. He cemented the fact that I needed to walk away from the Bible study site I held to so tightly. God initially guided me to this path, but instead of walking it for His glory, it became a Band-Aid to cover up a big wound. The wound played a broken soundtrack in my head, telling me I needed to prove myself in order to hold value. When these thoughts intruded, my grip tightened, and I worked harder to control the outcome. My heart feared what would happen without the safety of that Band-Aid.

Yet, I couldn't deny it. God was asking me to step into a quiet life with nothing in my hands. To walk away from something I had worked on so hard.

Over the next few months, wrapped in God's gentle leading and my husband's patient care, I released the death grip on my plans and surrendered to God's. I vowed to uncover my motivations and seek the Spirit's direction each day. I needed to put an end to the bad habit of plowing along at all costs. Good things done with the wrong motives do not bring freedom to us or glory to God — they only strangle the life out of us.

Courage doesn't always look like accomplishing some tremendous feat. Sometimes it's facing the fears in the dark corners of our hearts with hands open, asking God to give and take as He sees fit. It's incredibly scary to let go of control and trust God.

I won't lie. I grieved this long after I decided it. That first courageous step didn't feel victorious. No anthems played, heralding my brave decision. It actually felt a lot like loss. My empty hands seemed bad. I didn't understand how letting go of something I had worked on so hard could be good. Instead of walking in a victory parade, I felt like a coward slinking away from something important.

I shared this inner struggle with a friend. I told her I had let go of the Bible study site as an act of obedience to God's guidance, but I still had dreams in my heart. She said something that stopped me in my tracks.

"It sounds like an adventure."

That simple phrase entirely changed my perspective. For once in my life, adventure sounded fun. Instead of loss, I realized I gained something far better.

A well-loved Bible verse floated through my head, backing what my friend said: *For I, the LORD your God, will hold your right hand, saying to you, 'Fear not, I will help you'* (Isa. 41:13 NKJV).

When I released the control strangling the life out of me, I gained a path of freedom and beauty. God filled the space created by loss with His warm hand, leading me on a breathtaking and beautiful adventure.

Adventures are exciting. It seems like most people would jump right in at the mention of adventure. I wondered why I never saw them as good before. A quick internet search tells me the definition of *adventure* is to "engage in hazardous and exciting activity, especially the exploration of unknown territory."

What always tripped me up with adventures was the *hazardous, unknown territory* part. As a cautious person I prefer safe, controlled paths, thank you very much.

Fear told me control made more sense than risk. Control told me to avoid the path that looked rocky and steep. These flawed protective mechanisms told me to forge ahead on the safe path. One where I could predict what was coming in order to avoid hazards.

Ironically, in my attempts to walk the path that looked safer, I became more rigid and breakable by trying to be strong enough by myself.

Embarking on an adventure with God means we don't control the results. We can't predict what tomorrow will bring. We don't have the power to clear a path for miles. Instead, we take one step at a time. It means holding onto nothing but His gentle hand.

When I finally found the courage to unclench my fists, I enjoyed the genuine comfort and security that comes from God's hand alone. Between the first courageous step to surrender and my friend helping me see adventure in a new light, a different fire flickered to life in my chest. One that couldn't wait to follow God on whatever path He had. Instead of trying to avoid the hard, I now looked for the thrill. When my frantic efforts to succeed ceased, I could see God's mighty hand preparing the way.

The pressure to stay on the safe route leaves with the knowledge that hazards are a part of every journey. With God in the lead, He will break anything that threatens to break us. We can find courage in this truth when God interrupts our smooth path with a gentle tug. Turning our gaze to follow where He points, we see a steep and overgrown trail leading up the side of a mountain.

Fear instantly pulls at our heart and asks, "What's wrong with this flat route? It looks much safer." We teeter between adventure and "safety." Will we stubbornly proceed ahead on the flat path, dragging God along? After all, He promised He would never leave us. Or will we let Him gently guide us on the steep trail, trusting Him to clear a way, keep us safe, and show us some amazing things on the way up?

Each time we choose to follow God on these detours, it becomes easier to take those scary steps. We can walk this path of freedom and faith, knowing beauty waits around each bend.

I'm glad I took that courageous step to walk away from the Bible study site. That site was part of my journey, and I don't regret it, but it wasn't the path I needed to continue walking on. God had a new adventure waiting. After a period of rest, God led me to writing fiction. It was a path I would have tugged God past if I had remained too stubborn to surrender my plans.

Here I am, wildly loving this adventure. Yes, it's still scary. Often, I have no clue what my next step is. I still stub my toe and it hurts but, goodness, it's free and it's beautiful. Most of all, it's safe because I am holding the hand that holds me.

Courage is moving forward and grasping God's hand tighter than the fear that is trying to grip you.

Adventure is on the Other Side of Fear

What adventure is God beckoning you on? Will you be courageous enough to take the first step past fear and follow Him?

– 18 –

In My Eyes
Heather Popish

In my eyes, your courage is bigger than mine.

Your courage is louder and stronger.

You use it to climb mountains, swim oceans, and conquer the world.

My courage feels timid and small.

Courage is easier said than done.

Courage is having strength when facing the terrifying parts of life.

Courage is sometimes elusive; just out of my grasp.

Courageous is the last word I would pick to describe myself.

But I've learned that courage is picking up the pieces and moving on.

Courage is what you see on your child's face when they fall, yet get up and try again.

Courage wasn't meant to be easy,

but God commands us to be strong and courageous.

I need to stop playing the superhero, my cape fluttering as I try to save the world. Again.

I need to forgive that person who hurt me. Again.

I need to bite my tongue when it wants to lash out. Again.

When I feel I have failed God and myself,

courage is what I use to try again to look more like Jesus.

> *Haven't I commanded you: be strong and courageous? Do not be afraid or discouraged, for the Lord your God is with you wherever you go (Josh. 1:9 HCSB).*

– 19 –
Moonlight Kisses
Michele Marie Weisman

Every good action and every perfect gift is from God. These good gifts come down from the Creator of the sun, moon, and stars. God does not change like their shifting shadows
(James 1:17 ICB).

Five-year-old Rilee woke to duck-like squawking. Swimming further under her daisy embroidered comforter, she searched for quiet at the foot of her bed. *The baby*, Rilee thought, as the quacks turned into cries.

She tugged at the blankets, exposing one ear to her enemy. The darkness. The next cry came as a shrill pushing of the tide of her sleepiness. Drawing back under her sheets, a faint light peeked through a rippling at the edge of the fabric. *Where was the light coming from?*

The moonlight, Rilee gasped, seeing shadows turn her familiar things into monsters. Daring to glance further around her room, holding her breath, she identified each shadow. Dresser. Check. Toy box. Check. Basket full of stuffed animals. Check. Tennis shoes left out from yesterday. Check. Recognizing everything in her space, she exhaled.

I sound like Mommy with her grocery list, she thought while slipping out of bed. An iridescent path shone from the moon to her parent's bedroom door. *I will borrow the moon's light to be brave.*

Across the hall she faced the doorknob on her parent's bedroom door. Turning the knob meant the possibility of waking her mother. *Mommy's going to think I'm sneaking into her bed.*

She had been told night after night, "No more sleeping in our bed, Sweetie. You are a big girl now."

Another cry rang out from inside the room. Reaching up for the cold doorknob, heart racing, she held her breath and squeezed her eyelids shut as she turned the knob. It made no noise at being rotated. She opened her eyes and the door gently and obediently opened as she pushed. Just as quietly, she closed the door after entering the room.

A new cry spouted into the night.

Why isn't Mommy waking up? She saw the moon's light upon her parents' faces. The curtains were not drawn. Her eyebrows almost collided across her brow.

Daddy always closes those tight, thought Rilee. Nearing their bed, her eyes adjusting, she saw the outline of her parents.

Rilee moved toward the moon-lit bassinet.

The moon woke her. Moon, babies need sleep! Tilting her head toward the window, she scrunched up her eyes and pinched her lips. The bright sphere hung in the sky, wrapped by an unending silver cloud.

Stop moon! I don't mean to be rude, but you have to go. Rilee crept around the big bed to her father's side. She stretched tall in front of the window, grabbing at the curtains to seal them. The fabric could not meet at the very top, leaving a sliver of the moon still getting through.

Last night's laughter seemed to fill the room as she thought of her daddy chasing her and swinging her up into his arms. She turned to look at him. His sudden buzzing snore reminded her she had a job to do. *Help baby sister.*

As if on cue, a howl shattered the quiet.

Baby was gasping now, with loud cries between breaths. Rilee's heart drummed within her chest. She jumped at her reflection in the full-length mirror across from the bed. Taped upon it was a Sunday School coloring page with a drawing of the world.

"The Lord has the whole world in His hands," the teacher had told them.

Rilee relaxed at the memory of sitting by her best friend in class, reaching for the blue and green crayons to color the oceans and land. *He must have really big hands*, she recalled thinking.

She realized the cries from the baby had stopped. A sudden coo escaped from the bassinet. *Was she falling back to sleep? Maybe pushing the moonlight out helped!*

A *huff* came from the other side of the bedroom door. Rilee stiffened, like the neighbor's cat when hunting. Her hands flew to cover her mouth. Her eyes swamped with tears.

She often heard her daddy say, *Think, John, think*, when working on projects around the house.

"Think, Rilee, think," she whispered. Her hands slowly lowered. "Think *harder*, Rilee," she said through clenched teeth as her tears stopped.

Another huff drifted under the door, turning into a long sigh that ended with a jingle. Rilee almost laughed out loud. It was their Australian Shepherd, dog tags now resting on his paws, the familiar sound made when he laid down.

Silly Jasper thinks it is time to wake up. He must have heard the baby, too. She could almost feel his wet nose on her cheek. *Please don't paw the door, Jasper. Mommy, might not need to be woken.*

Turning her attention back to the crib, she stole toward the bassinet. *One, two, maybe three tippy toes more.*

Out of the corner of her eye she started again at her reflection in the large mirror. *Don't freeze. If Baby is asleep, Mommy and Daddy won't wake. What if Jasper's collar jingles when I leave?* Pinching her lips and scrunching her brow, she stooped a bit while inching toward the lovely white bassinet. Her family tells her she once slept in it, too. Eyelet fabric encircled the tiny crib, and the half-awning moonlight was shining upon it.

Rilee was near enough now to peek at her sister. She rubbed her eyes. *Where is baby?* She blinked and looked again. There was no baby.

Whaah, whaah. The cries were louder now, combined with sobbing.

"No! No! Baby," Rilee tried to yell.

"Honey. Honey. Wake up, Rilee." She felt her mother's arms rocking her gently.

Rilee opened her eyes, discovering they were both in her room. "Why are we on my bed?" She gasped between her words.

"Sweetie, you had a bad dream," Mother said, pulling Rilee closer into her embrace.

"The baby ... I was looking for the baby." Tears

streamed down Rilee's small cheeks as she breathed in her mother's familiar lavender lotion.

"Oh, honey." The moon half hid her mother's face.

Rilee, taking a deep breath amidst her sobs, reached out her hands and gently touched her mother's tummy, flooded with the memory of what happened, and what could have been. "Baby is with Jesus."

"Yes." Her mother cried without a sound, tiny splashes on Rilee's arm disclosing the night's secret.

"My heart hurts so much, Mommy." Rilee looked up, searching for her mother's eyes.

"Mine, too." She breathed deeply, as if attempting to slow the flow of her own tears. "We'll get through this together … you, me, and Daddy."

Jasper wedged between the two, pushing his wet nose onto the young girl's cheek and licking away her tears. A giggle rang out as his soft fur feathered her neck. Her mother steadied a smile in the moonlight.

"Jasper has the right idea." She bent forward to kiss Rilee's forehead and glimpsed the moon's light upon it. "Well, it looks like the dog and the moon kissed you before me. I'm next!"

"Oh, Mommy," Rilee giggled under the tender kiss, a balm to her heart.

Her mother sang softly, "He's got the whole world in his hands," as the tide of sleep returned to Rilee.

– 20 –
Under One Condition
Libby Taylor-Worden

I hung up the phone and peeked into my boss's office. "May I take a few hours off? I need to go to the hospital." The expression on his face made it clear that I likely looked as pale as I felt, stunned and uncertain.

"Are you okay?" he inquired.

"I'm fine, I just . . ."

"Sit down." He rose and motioned to the chair in his office.

Unsure if I could walk to the chair, I chose to remain standing. "I'm good. I took a call from my church. There's a woman in the hospital asking for me by name. I barely know her. I just met her over the weekend."

"And she's asking for you? Is she ... dying?"

"Sorry, she's not *in* the hospital, she's *at* the hospital. Her daughter is dying. They think she has only a few hours to live."

"Well, of course. Go. Take all the time you need."

"But Greg, I don't even know her or her daughter. And ... I've never done anything like this before ... death, I mean." I couldn't get the pleading out of my voice. Even though I had agreed to go, I was still looking for a way out, an excuse to keep me from walking into the biggest unknown of my life.

Greg was a man of faith, a sort of shepherd of the believers in our office. So, although I was asking my boss for time off, I was really begging for insight as to how I should handle the situation. I could feel my face pinched with longing, waiting for him to tell me what to do.

"What do I say?"

"God will give you the words." He returned his look to his work.

I collected my things and left for the hospital, praying with every breath I took. My prayers were more a laundry list of requests with very little listening for God to answer. I arrived in the hospital parking lot. *Okay, God. I'll do this under one condition. You have to tell me what to say. You have to give me the words. I have no idea how to do this.*

Under One Condition

Our associate pastor met me in the waiting area. Suzie was sitting like a rag doll, hunched over, staring at her hands, not even crying. The pastor motioned me to her side. I sat next to her and laid my hand on her arm to let her know I was there. She looked up, but only a brief flash of recognition acknowledged I had come in response to her request. A meager smile twitched at the corner of her mouth and quickly vanished.

God, now would be a good time ... what do I say? No words came to me. Not one.

My heart was bursting with compassion for this young woman. It had been explained to me that she had put her twin girls down for a nap. A while later she had responded to one of the girls who was crying wildly. When she entered the room, she discovered her other daughter hanging by her neck. She had crawled out of her crib and gotten a toy wrapped around her neck, caught on the top of the crib's railing. The toy that had gone missing that morning must have been tucked into the mattress of the crib.

I opened my mouth, half wanting to speak but nothing came out. *God, help.* Still nothing. I wrapped one arm around her shoulders and we sat there in silence until a nurse motioned for us to go into the room where her daughter lay.

I led Suzie into the room, half holding her up as we walked. The lights were bright, illuminating the gray walls, gray floor, and gray equipment. Only a slight smell of hospital lingered in the air. Equipment was strategically positioned around the room, yet none of it was connected to the tiny body lying on the large bed, except the single heart monitor with blips coming at long, erratic intervals. The nurse whispered to me, "Her body temperature has dropped, she only has a few minutes."

Still no words came. Still, I remained silent.

I longed to add some comfort or insight or encouragement, but had no idea what to say. We sat in the chairs they provided and the nurse carefully placed the small, nearly-lifeless body into Suzie's arms. She dimmed the lights and left the room.

Tears streamed down my cheeks, yet Suzie sat in a daze, dry eyed. I wasn't sure she was even aware of what was happening. She stroked her daughter's cheek and brushed a blond hair from her forehead. The 18-month-old was tightly swaddled in a blanket not unlike a newborn when first handed to its mother following its birth. Only one arm free from the blanket with the monitor attached. She lay peacefully with the residual marks on her face where tubes had been taped to her tiny mouth. Her relaxed lips slightly parted, all rosy color gone.

I doubt Suzie noticed these details. She rocked her daughter. Or was she just rocking, a nervous response to the situation?

I don't know how long we sat there. It felt like an hour, but was more likely ten minutes when the nurse came in again. I looked up but Suzie remained staring into the face of her daughter.

"She's gone. You need to put her back on the bed," the nurse whispered. "I'll give you a minute."

The nurse slipped out. I glanced at the monitor — no more blips. How was I going to get Suzie to release her daughter for the last time? How was I going to tell her that her daughter was dead? *I'm not good at this, God. I need your help.* We sat in silence a couple of minutes as I held Suzie's shoulders. The nurse appeared in the doorway and I knew she was beckoning me to take action.

I turned and spoke for the first time. "It's over, let's put her to bed." *Where did that idea come from?* The words had just come out of my mouth.

Suzie rose and gently place her daughter on the bed. She covered her with a blanket as if she was putting her down for a nap. Suzie stroked her cold arm once more and turned to look at me, her eyes pleading for someone to make sense of what was happening.

When we left the room, she turned for a last look at her daughter. I didn't need to tell Suzie her daughter was gone. Her shoulders rolled forward and she dug her head into my arm as I wrapped my arms around her. We made our way back to the waiting room.

Many things happened in the next hour. The pastor handled everything. When someone came for Suzie, I released her but I couldn't stop praying that God would wrap His loving arms around her and support her. I prayed God would give her the words to somehow explain to her other daughter what her future would be like—a twin, alone.

Drained of energy, I barely knew what to do next. I retrieved my purse and coat, but then the pastor returned. "Thank you for coming, you handled that perfectly."

"What?" My eyes must have been asking for more of an explanation.

He continued, "She didn't need anyone to quote scripture or tell her everything would work out for the best. She just needed someone to sit with her, to hold her."

On the drive home the events of the day ran through my mind like an instant replay, over and over again. Understanding dawned. *Thank You, God, for keeping my mouth shut.*

– 21 –
Courage vs. Wisdom
Malcolm Mackinnon

"Open box before eating pizza!"

You wouldn't think anyone really needed to be told this, but it didn't stop one particular company from printing these words on its packaging.

During the Sermon on the Mount, Jesus also gives what, at first, appears to be a pointless piece of advice. He tells His hearers: *Do not throw your pearls to pigs* (Matt. 7:6 NIV). Since it's doubtful anyone would ever do this, why does Jesus say it?

Jesus never gives pointless advice. He's giving an illustration connected to what He has just been talking about. He has been explaining that we are not to be judgmental, specifically when judging others in a hypocritical way. However, from this many have wrongly concluded we are never to make any kind of judgment at all.

That's not the case. Jesus is exhorting us to make sound judgments, to introduce wise reasoning and advice, even rebuke, into situations where they are needed. The whole focus of the sermon has been for God's people to raise their bar of understanding and to see themselves as the ambassadors of Christ.

We are God's representatives. We are called to function in the society around us as those who are merciful, pure in heart, peacemakers, who hunger and thirst for righteousness, and who are meek (Matt. 5:5-9 NIV). Why? Because these are all the attributes of Christ Himself. In this way we advertise the living God who has not only changed us, but who seeks to reveal Himself through us to those who still need to find Him.

Immediately after saying these things, Jesus reminds His hearers they are the light of the world (Matt. 5:14-16 NIV). God has lit a lamp within us which needs to be seen. He warns us to not hide that light, but to make sure it can shine and be visible.

So, He gives us pearls. A pearl is a precious and valuable gemstone, a symbol of purity and perfection.

Pearls are considered beautiful and are used to enhance a person's appearance. In the context here, our pearls refer to the good characteristics, habits, and outward demonstrations of God's love that we naturally have through being connected to Christ.

The Parable of the Pearl in Matthew 13 speaks of a merchant seeking the greatest pearl: *Again, the kingdom of heaven is like a merchant looking for fine pearls. When he found one of great value, he went away and sold everything he had and bought it* (Matt. 13:45-46 NIV).

The analogy is about finding Jesus. Jesus *is* the pearl of great price. When we discover Jesus, and what He has done for us, we give up everything for Him. Just as physical pearls enhance a person's beauty, so Christ adorns us in spiritual beauty so that His beauty might be seen through us.

Have you ever wondered why Christ speaks of pearls instead of, say, gold or diamonds? Among the world's gemstones the pearl is unique as being the only one that grows inside a living organism. The illustration is specific to the work of Christ causing His attributes to grow organically inside us as we remain close to Him.

We live in a world of insanity where all kinds of things are accepted as good which are clearly not. Sound judgment left the building a long time ago. We are now called to be the bearers of God's good judgment to our generation.

"Throwing" our pearls conjures a picture of violence. I prefer the versions that use the word "casting." It puts me more in mind of the sower going out to sow (or cast) the seed, with the emphasis on evangelizing, discipling, and growing the kingdom. Likewise, we have our pearls and we are to make them known to those around us.

And here's where courage is needed. It takes a lot to be prepared to cast our pearls, to believe a situation has arisen into which some godly wisdom needs to be introduced, and to be willing to be the channel through which the wisdom comes.

We should know from experience that reactions to our attempts to give spiritual insight can vary greatly. Our hearers might ignore us, pity us, dismiss us, or even become irritable with us. And, sometimes, those responses are enough to put us off trying. But God calls us to this for the precise reason there are some out there who will respond favorably to what we tell them. The Old Testament encourages us: *Like an earring of gold or an ornament of fine gold is the rebuke of a wise judge to a listening ear* (Prov. 25:12 NIV).

Remember, there are still some out there with *a listening ear* who want to hear God's opinion. And our courage in being prepared to tell them might just be the catalyst through which they enter the Kingdom of God.

If any of this sounds daunting, it's always worth reminding ourselves of another great theme of the Sermon on the Mount. We are not only being called to a standard of life and behavior that Christ would exhibit, we are also given His Holy Spirit to be able to do the things we can't naturally do ourselves.

But here's where Jesus makes His point: there are some people before whom we should *not* share the things of God. More than that, He calls them pigs (or swine) and dogs. What is the significance of these two animals? These descriptions are used of people who are senseless to the things of God and who have no appreciation or ability to receive instruction from Christ. As such, Jesus warns His hearers and us that we are not to give them the benefit of our wisdom. He says this to not only warn us about the futility of trying to communicate with certain people, He also wants to protect us from possible retaliation.

There are those for whom sharing our pearls is waste of time. We only have a limited amount of time and opportunities. Why waste those openings on people whose ears are already closed? Some will steal our pearls. They will wear us out, strip our assets, make us feel disenchanted, and rob us of the desire to ever attempt anything for God again.

But Jesus also reminds us of those who are not just indifferent to our message, but who will be actively hostile against it. Now, any Christian service comes with danger. We're involved in a spiritual battle and not everyone will like what we do. But Jesus goes on to mention the potential violent response from some people. Jesus talks about the pigs trampling on the pearls and the dogs being capable of turning on us. The Bible doesn't speak about dogs as housetrained pets, but as packs of wild animals ready to tear people to pieces.

A person could argue that being prepared to die is actually a part of our Christian outlook. Some are called to be martyrs, and both the Bible and the accounts of church history record the final days of many who stood their ground before being killed for their faith.

But here's the difference. Jesus is advising us not to put ourselves deliberately in situations of danger. He cautions us to be aware of those not only disinterested in our words, but who are seeking violent reprisals upon us for trying to bring our pearls into their life.

God desires the safety of His people. He declares His protection and guidance over us, He goes with us

Courage vs. Wisdom

through all our valley experiences, and doesn't want us to be needlessly exposed to the fury of those who could destroy us.

Amid our courage we need great wisdom. Many times, Jesus would not speak to the Pharisees or answer their questions. His silence had nothing to do with cowardice, but with realizing His words would fall on deaf ears. Look at how He answered Pilate and Herod in Luke 23. Jesus answered Pilate because He saw him as an inquirer of the truth. However, with Herod, He said nothing, knowing Herod cared nothing for God.

Jesus could make a quick diagnosis of all those before Him, and knew the difference between the sheep and the pigs. He could pick up the clues which revealed those who had an interest in His words, and those who didn't. He gives us His Holy Spirit that we might have the same discernment.

With this in mind, let us modify a famous old prayer:

Lord, give us the courage to cast our pearls.
Give us the wisdom to know when to be silent.
And give us the insight to know the difference.

– 22 –
God, Courage, and Toilet Paper
Debbie Jones Warren

All was quiet in the fourth-grade hall after Lights Out in the girls' dorm near the village of Miango, Nigeria. However, on that night in the spring of 1969, the four of us in my bedroom at the boarding school for missionaries' children held a serious conversation.

"There's an uprising going on," one girl whispered from the top bunk.

I sat up and hung my legs over the side of my bed. "What's an uprising?"

"It's a war. The Nigerians in the south are fighting with the ones in the north."

"Are we in danger here at Kent Academy? I think we're in the center of the country," I said.

"No. The fighting isn't close, so we're safe at KA," the first girl replied.

My best friend Joyce spoke up from the lower bunk across the room. "Today I heard two of the dorm uncles talking." A ray of moonlight streamed through the slit in the curtain and shone on her calm face. "The men were making plans to help everyone leave KA if we need to."

"That sounds scary," the girl above me said.

"If we have to run away, where will we go?" My voice wobbled a little.

"We're not going anywhere," Joyce said. "The uncles saw me listening and told me not to worry. They said their plan was just a precaution, and we are all safest staying right here."

"What's a precaution?" I didn't feel too comforted.

"The uncles explained that they're just being very careful." Joyce's quiet voice was reassuring. "I think it's all very interesting, and I'm not frightened one bit."

Lying back, I tried to calm down, but I kept tossing and turning. I remembered the Bible verse we read in devotions after dinner: *Be strong and of good courage; do not be afraid, nor be dismayed, for the LORD your God is with you wherever you* go (Josh. 1:9 NKJV.)

"Dear Jesus, please be with my family wherever they go." Finally, I drifted off to sleep.

News from Home

The next morning after breakfast, Joyce and I crossed the playground toward the single-story school building. Along the way, we stepped on each hopscotch square painted on the tarmac. Then we strolled past the tall mango tree with its shady leaves.

Already the bright African sun warmed my skin comfortingly, and I pushed lingering thoughts of war to the back of my mind. I needed to concentrate on my classwork.

But at lunch, my tummy knotted up when I smelled the food on my plate. The Nigerian stew with rice was one of my favorite dishes. After the first few bites, I couldn't swallow past the worry that stuck in my throat.

Later, in my bedroom for our daily afternoon rest hour, my tummy settled. Soon the dorm mother walked through the hallway and handed out mail.

"Here's something for Debbie Jones," she said with a smile.

"Yay! I got a letter from home!" As I read Mom's neat handwriting, I could hear her voice as if she were sitting on the bed next to me. "There is fighting in the south, and the war is moving closer to us here at Egbe. But don't worry about Dad and me."

My fingers shook as I read that last sentence and tears brimmed in my eyes. I blinked quickly and pushed on. "We keep a suitcase packed so we can escape into the jungle at a moment's notice."

Suddenly, my stomach clenched again, and worried thoughts buzzed like a swarm of bees in my brain. *Will my family be safe if they run away? How can they fit all their important things into just one case?*

Clutching the letter in one hand, I rolled to my side, faced the wall, and traced my fingers in circles over the tiny bumps in the cool cement. *How would they even manage?*

The Important Things

Lying there, I pictured the scene. My parents marching along a narrow, dirt path through the tall brush behind our house. Dad in his familiar khaki slacks and loose, cotton shirt, clutching a heavy suitcase. Mom wearing her favorite red tennis shoes and a knee-length skirt and scurrying behind him. She was cradling baby Cindy in her left arm while clinging to three-year-old Grant with her right hand.

I bolted upright and faced the other set of bunk beds. "Listen to this, roomies! My parents are near the danger and might have to run away. Mommy says they've packed a suitcase and are prepared to escape."

"Oh dear!" The girl across from me looked worried.

I took a deep breath. "I'm scared for them. But mostly, I wonder how much they can fit into one suitcase. And what on earth should they pack?"

"I think they should take a lot of undies," one roommate said.

"Maybe they can bring some food," another girl suggested.

"They'll need a Bible, of course," said Joyce.

I leaned back on my pillow and stared at the mattress springs of the bunk above me. "Well, I really think they should fill it with toilet paper! Otherwise, they won't be able to go to the bathroom."

My legs started itching like they usually did when I felt sweaty. Lying back down, I scratched vigorously and thought some more. *Mommy could probably fit six rolls in one suitcase. That should last a while.*

Silently I said a short prayer. *God, please take care of them and give them courage.*

"Debbie, I know you're worried," Joyce said. "But I believe our families are all going to be okay. I'll pray for your parents every day."

"Thanks. That makes me feel better," I said.

Finally, I had a happy thought: *I'm glad my brother Larry is safe here with me. And little Mark is, too.*

I heaved a sigh and settled down to rest. *When school is done this afternoon, I'll look for them on the playground and give both of my brothers a big hug.*

Looking Back

After Nigeria gained independence from the British in October 1960, three provinces were formed along tribal lines. However, the Hausa, Yoruba, and Igbo peoples struggled to get along because of long-standing tribal tensions.

In July 1967, the Igbo in the southeast declared their independence as the Republic of Biafra. That started the Nigerian Civil War, also known as the Biafran War, which raged throughout the country until January 1970. Fortunately, the fighting never reached our village of Egbe or our boarding school at Miango.

When I Facetimed with my mom about this memory, she added a crucial detail: "Kent Academy was targeted by Igbos because they wanted to take it over as a sanctuary. I don't know how the mission board kept them out of the school compound."

That explained the conversation my friend Joyce overheard between the two dorm fathers. If the Igbos had overtaken the Kent Academy compound, the staff and students would have had to evacuate.

Then I asked Mom the all-important question: "What did you have in that suitcase? While at school, I worried that you'd need a lot of toilet paper."

She laughed. "I packed a change of clothes for each of us and a lot of cloth diapers!"

* * *

In March 2020, we had to shelter in place to slow the spread of COVID-19. In the stores, many items became scarce, and the most memorable among them was toilet paper. When new shipments arrived, people stocked up, some to the point of hoarding.

Even with all the restrictions throughout 2020, I felt peaceful and happy to do my part, because I'd lived through other critical situations in my lifetime. For example, in Nigeria our family had experienced a Lassa fever outbreak, running out of missionary funds midterm, and getting lost in the rainforest. Although each difficulty was different, I'd seen God's faithfulness in the past, and that helped me cope in the present.

When I first heard toilet paper was in short supply, I traveled back in my mind to this childhood memory and again felt the uncertainty of it all. Yet, I remembered how, as a nine-year-old, I learned to trust God and take courage from family and friends—even if we ran out of toilet paper.

> *You will not fear the terror of night, nor the arrow that flies by day ... nor the plague that destroys at midday ... For he will command his angels concerning you to guard you in all your ways (Ps. 91:5-11 NIV).*

– 23 –
The Doors
Lenette Lindsey

There I stood, waiting with my dad behind those dark, heavy, tall, wooden doors listening to the orchestra play Pachelbel's "Canon in D Major." Through the crack between the closed double doors, faded colored light shone. My dad stood next to me in a tux — the relaxed, easy-going physician, bass fiddle-playing, guitar-strumming, country singer dad. I'd never seen him dress so sharp in all my life.

The music stopped, and silence filled the air for what seemed like an eternity. A majestic feeling surrounded the old English-style chapel. All I had planned, imagined, and wanted was about to become a reality. I waited in a beautiful white gown. Its capped sleeves dropped just below my shoulders. Voluminous and airy, my tulle dress brushed against anyone who walked within four feet of it. My hair formed a bun that rested within a pearl crown on my head. Even Cinderella, in her most glorious moment, would have been jealous. The setting was perfect and regal. Only a door separated me from the rest of my life. *But wait. What is so majestic about marriage?* At such an inopportune moment, I internalized racing thoughts of common marriage expressions. Butterfly wings were dancing in my stomach. *I'm about to take the plunge, bite the dust, and lose my freedom.* The terms merged with truths, albeit negative truths. *Marriage is challenging. It's a lot of work. Twenty-five percent or more of all marriages fail, even among Christians.*[1] If mountain-climbing on the side of a cliff in Colorado or hopping into a woven basket tied with ropes to a gigantic balloon had a twenty-five percent failure rate, would I choose those? Courageously, I had experienced both high adrenaline activities. But if my odds were one in four

---

[1] Feldhaun, Shaunti. "Divorce Rates Are Not What You Think They Are." *Shaunti.com*, 27 May 2021, https://shaunti.com/2021/05/divorce-rates-are-not-what-you-think-they-are/.

that I'd plunge into the valley beneath the mountain, or my basket would go up in flames in midair, then no way. Committing the rest of your life to someone takes courage. There's no anticipation of foiled matrimony, yet one-fourth or more end in divorce. For some, stepping out of a destructive marriage is the most courageous choice. The odds for a successful marriage are scary. How would we beat the odds? Could I answer that question in the next second or two before I heard the familiar *dum, dum, da-dum* and the doors to the rest of my life opened?

Memories like a rewound videotape flashed before my eyes. My retrospection confirmed that Joel was the one, but could I actually go through those doors? I saw myself walking out of the door of my apartment just ten months earlier on my way to my church's singles' Christmas party. Grumbling about how I didn't want to go, my roommate responded, "Go. You'll have a good time and probably meet the man you're going to marry."

"Yeah, right. That's not going to happen," I said, and closed the door behind me. Getting married was the last thing on my mind.

My roommate was right, and my husband-to-be waited just on the other side of those dark, heavy, tall, wooden doors. Joel Lindsey, the man who glanced across the room a few times at that party and smiled the most charming smile anyone could imagine, awkwardly but so innocently, made his first introduction. The apartment, crowded with shoulder-to-shoulder people, proved challenging. Therefore, he positioned himself so I'd bump into him. "Hi. I'm Joel," he proclaimed. I can't even remember all we talked about that night, but the next hour flew by, and it was time to go home. Not knowing if I would ever see him again, I said, "Well, maybe I'll see you at church sometime." Then I left. He overheard me give my number to another person at the party, memorized it, and called me the next night. We set our first date for the following weekend.

The condensed but fruitful months that followed justified a spring break trip to take Joel home to meet my parents. We flew to Washington State, and upon arrival, my brother's wife summoned me to go out for some girl time. A little suspicious, I left Joel to visit with my parents, who he had just met an hour before. I later found out he prearranged this. From his perspective, he jumped off the plane, extended his hand for a friendly shake, and said to my parents, "Hi, I'm Joel, and I'd like to become a part of your family." In actuality, he talked to them for a couple of hours and traditionally asked for my hand in marriage.

The Doors

The next day we drove north into Canada and enjoyed a customary English high tea. A perfect Ms. Potts character, with an accent and bonnet, served our tea and crumpets. The colossal room echoed with endless high tea chatter. "Life just doesn't get any better than this!" I said as we sipped tea at the Empress Hotel in Victoria. Joel, a timely man, took advantage of the moment. He knelt on one knee beside my chair. Reaching into his pocket, he said, "Lenette, I love you very much and want to spend the rest of my life with you. Will you marry me?"

After my yes, the beautiful ring, the tears, the hugs, the pictures, and Ms. Potts refilling our teapot, two older ladies in conventional tea attire, including their fascinators, approached our table. One said to Joel in an English accent, "Young man, until today, we did not know chivalry still existed." I loved this moment. And our proper English friends were not wrong; he was chivalrous.

That same chivalrous man stood on the other side of those dark, heavy, tall, wooden doors awaiting my arrival. Would his courage to ask for my hand in marriage and wait at the altar be met with mine to walk through those doors? I knew honorable and courteous behavior displayed by knights was easy for both of us with others watching. How would chivalry play out in the middle of an argument or awakened by a newborn at two o'clock in the morning?

    I'd recently found an article my mother-in-law gave me just before the wedding. It was written from a balanced perspective of the vows that young love often overlooks. For better or worse, for richer or poorer, in sickness and in health, until death do us part. The article gave brilliant advice to naïve couples plunging into marriage bliss who probably aren't thinking about the crises that often arise in family life. It gave examples of what crises will do to a marriage and relationship prescriptions for how to walk through them. But what stood out to me was the section on spiritual resources—namely faith, God's Word, and support from other believers. In that section, the right-hand column of the article cut off as she photocopied it. My mother-in-law took time to fill in the words that had disappeared at the end of each line all the way down the page. In the most important part of the article, she was bridging the gap between the ignorant bliss of newlyweds and the faith-filled fortitude of mature Christian couples who would undoubtedly experience troubled times. She had been through some crises in relationships herself and wanted to impart God-given truth and wisdom before we said I do.

The Doors

The proposal took courage, the yes took courage, the showing up at the altar took courage, and the walking through those dark, heavy, tall, wooden doors would also take courage. But the genuine test of courage would come in the daily life of being married. Forgive daily as I have been forgiven, show patience as God has shown patience with me, be selfless as Jesus laid down His life for me, and choose kindness even when it's hard. To bear the image of Christ and His bride within our marriage would take utter dependence on the One who brought us together.

Courageous faith in God carried us through difficult first years—near divorce, infertility, adoption, financial struggles, and even the death of our child. Blessings, bliss, and laughter have also been a part of our journey. The answer to the question, "How would we beat the odds?" became clearer with time, experience, wisdom, prayer, and a lot of grace. Indeed, it will continue to take all those things until death do us part. In courage, I stood at the door and knocked. God made an open door for me which no one can shut. Even when I was weak, my faith in His Word was strong. Today, I continue to rely on His Word as I ask for strength in His powerful name for my marriage and all the challenges in family life. My marriage is more about Him than it is about me. When those dark, heavy, tall, wooden doors opened twenty-six years ago, I courageously stepped into the rest of my life.

– 24 –
When the Itsy Bitsy Spider Isn't
Debra Celovsky

She wanted to sing her new song.

My two-year-old granddaughter stood in the living room twisting her toddler fingers into climby-spider shapes. Most adults discover that "The Itsy Bitsy Spider" is a tune with which one must sing along, and I did.

However, we also discovered that Itsy was not in our collection of children's books. This meant going on a quest in the next few days for a colorful board book about the critter. I found one, glanced through it, liked the creative illustrations, and brought it home. Natalia, as it happened, was spending the night. I showed her the book, anticipating her delight. Instead, a slight frown, then a wary smile.

"Do you want me to read it to you?" I asked her before bedtime.

"No."

Later, she awakened out of a sound sleep sobbing, "No itsy bitsy spider!"

The book quickly disappeared from her library, consigned to a spot high on top of the bookshelf.

I thought about what had just happened.

It does seem like an odd thing to tell a child: "This spider, sweetheart, is insane. He keeps doing the same thing over and over again while expecting a different result." Plus, I was also pathologically afraid of spiders as a child, and am not exactly crazy about them as an adult.

I decided to do some quick research on arachnids. Oh, my. The illustrations were graphic, including closeups of *spider faces!* Was that really necessary? The claim was made that, while there are thirty thousand known kinds of spiders, very few can actually harm people. This was not a comfort.

I gave up on the creepy pictures and retrieved Natalia's reject. The first two pages were lines familiar to "Itsy Bitsy" readers everywhere: the waterspout, the rain, the sun. But turn the page and — *surprise!* We

When the Itsy Bitsy Spider Isn't

have a reason for Itsy's efforts: he has spun his web high on the rooftop for a better view of the landscape and is simply trying to get home. He dons goggles in a second attempt. He shields himself with an umbrella, bounces on a trampoline, detours across a clothesline. He's blown into a tree with angry birds.

Is he discouraged? No! He's clever! He's tenacious! He's courageous! And he has a great attitude. I took a giant mental leap and thought of a paraphrase of Churchill's famous lines that hung on the wall in my study: *Never, ever, ever give up.*

Itsy, as it turns out, is a pretty decent illustration of the way a robust faith operates ... looking at a huge setback or enormous task and saying, *I'm going to take God at His Word and endeavor to do the right thing and act with courage* (2 Chron. 19:11 NIV). Now there's something to plant in the heart of a child, or on which to plant your own spiritual flag.

Natalia and I had another go at Itsy when she was a little older—with a much better response. And it turned out to be one of those books that was handed down to the next little and the next, thankfully without the terror — or any more research.

– 25 –
The Courage to Share
Rebecca Mitchell

My daughter and I call them funnies—those silly, embarrassing mistakes that seldom cause harm except to our own egos. I've had my share of bathroom funnies.

One time, I walked into the usually unoccupied bathroom at work, chose the last of three stalls, glanced into the mirror as I turned, and exclaimed out loud, "Wow, my butt looks so big!" I sat down, and that's when I heard it: the loud rattling of the toilet paper roll. I was not alone. A few days later, I entered the same quiet bathroom, complained out loud, "Why is it always so smelly in here?" only to be met again with the dreaded toilet paper roll rattle in the next stall. I have since taken a vow of silence upon entering that bathroom lest my spontaneous utterances further mortify me.

My bathroom mortification doesn't end there, however. I accidentally went into the men's bathroom at the Mount Hermon writing conference, saw the urinals, and somehow imagined I had seen a temporary sign converting one of the men's bathrooms to accommodate all the women. Seems logical, even smart, right? Well, such was not the case. I was alone when I went in, but soon I was stuck in the stall with men coming and going (pun intended), including my instructor, I think. I didn't look too closely.

I share these stories with my daughter and my close friends so we can laugh together, commiserate on the stupid things we do, and sigh in relief that somebody else isn't perfect either. It doesn't take courage to share my funnies with them because I know they will laugh with me, not at me, and continue to love me despite my goofy mistakes. However, it does take courage to share more serious missteps, failures, sins, or struggles. It takes courage to admit to angry outbursts, jealousy, gossip, selfishness, affairs, or addictions. It takes courage to reveal where we stumble, but in vulnerable revelation with safe people and with God we can find freedom.

We've all been there. Regretting time wasted. Brooding about a tense conversation that we made worse by our reaction. Stewing over harsh words said to our kids. Ruminating on a wrong decision, from a bad paint color to a bad relationship. We often wish we could turn back the clock and have a do-over, a mulligan. But we can't. Instead, especially if the mistake is serious, we often have to take several courageous steps to deal with it, one of which is to share that mistake with others.

Some of the most courageous sharing I see is at DivorceCare, a faith-based support group for people going through separation or divorce. Walking in the door the first night, wearing a red "D" on my sweater — or so I felt — was admitting I had failed in my marriage. Once I got past the anger of what my ex-husband had done to break our bond, I had to take a hard look at myself to recognize my own mistakes, especially patterns of behavior, that had impacted the health of our marriage. I shared some of these mistakes with my group at DivorceCare and even more with my therapist and discovered something amazing: I wasn't alone. I was human. I was a sinner among sinners. What a relief!

Sharing our mistakes or struggles with a safe person or support community can give us the freedom to move forward instead of staying stuck in our guilt or shame. But why stop at sharing our struggles? If that sharing can bring relief and increase our ability to move on, what about sharing our heartaches? A career setback, a damaged relationship, a traumatic past, a lost child all can cause a deep, painful ache in our souls. Being vulnerable and sharing our heartaches with those who care and understand can bring comfort beyond expectations.

After the last series of DivorceCare, which I now co-lead, we asked for anonymous feedback from over fifty participants. One person commented, "Table time is super important. I need to be with others going through the same thing," confirming the benefit of sharing our struggles and heartaches. Another person wrote, "Less time Rebecca speaking, less control, and less seriousness." Ouch. This person's most specific suggestion about the whole program was to have me talk less. I already struggle with having confidence that God can use my introverted, reticent voice in front of a group, so this comment struck deeply. Throughout my life I've been told "You're so quiet," and I've struggled to assert my thoughts and ideas without beating myself up when they go a little sideways. And now I should talk even less? I confess I cried and wanted to stop speaking. Only when I shared the comment with others who helped me weigh it properly could I let it go and move on. And only now, as I share this with you, do I realize it's an accomplishment for me to go from "You're so quiet" to "Talk less."

As I talk more, I'm sharing my struggles and heartaches with trusted friends, but I still have trouble sharing my dreams. What if they sound ridiculous? What if I don't even make progress toward them? If I share a dream and then fail to achieve it, I'll be embarrassed, not only for failing but also for having the dream in the first place. However, the opposite is more likely to happen. If we share our dreams—dreams of writing a book, becoming an artist, starting a family, creating a business—we just might discover others with similar dreams who will pray and encourage us in ours.

When I first dreamt of writing a divorce recovery devotional and Bible study as a follow-up to DivorceCare, I was doubtful it could be done or, more accurately, that I could do it. Being the queen of unfinished projects, completing an entire book seemed as likely as a Krispy Kreme donut without any calories. Plus, who was I to write such a book? I didn't feel qualified, but I did feel compelled, so I shared with a few people who encouraged me to write, go to conferences, and share my dream with agents and editors. God's hand and grace fueled this dream: *From Broken Vows to Healed Hearts* was released May 22, 2018.

I've been advocating that we share our struggles, heartaches, and dreams with others, but we also benefit from sharing them with God. We could argue that He already perceives our thoughts from afar and is familiar with all our ways (Ps. 139:2–3 NIV), but speaking these things out loud to God makes them more tangible, more honest. Confessing our struggles brings forgiveness: *If we confess our sins, He is faithful and just and will forgive us our sins and purify us from all unrighteousness* (1 John 1:9 NIV). Lamenting our losses or heartaches brings healing: *May Your unfailing love be my comfort* (Ps. 119:76 NIV). Professing our dreams brings hope: *But now, Lord, what do I look for? My hope is in You* (Ps. 39:7 NIV). In my time with God, I've begun weekly journaling about a struggle, a heartache, and a dream. Whether small or large, revealing these parts of my soul with the Creator of my soul builds the intimacy and freedom I long for with God. Without such honest sharing, I'm not fully present, not fully me.

God is trustworthy for this intimate sharing, but some people are not. We should be courageous when communicating with others but not foolhardy. Unsafe people can use the information against us or tell others without our permission. Even well-meaning people can sting with obnoxious cliches or unsolicited advice. So, how do we determine who is safe and who isn't? Deciding by trial and error doesn't sound like a fun or safe proposition. Instead, we can proceed slowly by trusting in increments, looking for others going through similar circumstances, and seeking professional help when the issue is chronic or deep into our past. Most of all, we can pray for God's guidance as we share with others, and they, in turn, share with us.

We all have struggles. We all have heartaches. We all have dreams. May we have the courage to be vulnerable as we share these with others. Even more so, may we have the courage to accept God's invitation to come into His presence fully ourselves, without masks to hide our sin, accepting His tenderness in our heartache, and sharing our dreams for the future.

> *But God has surely listened and has heard my prayer. Praise be to God, who has not rejected my prayer or withheld His love from me!*
> *(Ps. 66:19–20 NIV)*

– 26 –
Courageous Love
Kimberly Novak

Growing up, Ivy was never a gutsy girl. Even now, she is definitely not a bold woman. Comfortably living in the shadows of others and being too shy for anything more, Ivy was willing to do whatever was necessary to keep those around her happy. However, Ivy faced a significant decision when her world unexpectedly turned upside down. She was forced to consider if she would live the second half of her life withdrawn, or finally become the courageous woman she was meant to be.

Ivy found herself in a situation unlike anything she had ever encountered and knew finding a way to triumph over her doubts was the only way to endure.

She struggled with the unknown of how she would transform her fear into courage, not to mention finding the nerve and confidence to let others see her as a brave woman. It never occurred to Ivy that a most prevalent blessing would emerge amid her most significant battle. It was in the quiet of her spirit where she met the One who would arouse a change. Some might see it as strange that the happenstance occurred only through thoughts and feelings. However, it is in the heart where love blooms ... and Ivy accepted the invitation.

In the turmoil of all that was going on, it was initially difficult to see the miracle staring her in the face. Because of this, Ivy held back through the initial stages of this newfound relationship, fraught with the idea of letting Him in. It was apparent that she needed to find the confidence she lacked to begin to reveal who she was inside. Because Ivy was a gal who thrived on creative expression, early conversations started with pen and paper. These writings included everything from hobbies and frustrations to the most intimate moments. Through maintaining consistency and daily communication, Ivy's confidence grew. Each encounter was a stepping stone and fed her desire to express her true self.

The written dialogue continued as Ivy muddled through her situation's ups and downs. Before long, she found herself wanting to open up. Willingly, and with some awkwardness, she journaled a heartfelt message indicating her hunger for a closer connection. Inhaling a deep breath, Ivy closed her prayer journal and rested the pen on the cover. Quietly and with eyes closed, she opened her hands. Instantly, her emotions were overpowering, leaving her feeling invigorated and alive. Knowing she was in His presence, Ivy held onto hope, sharing her innermost thoughts. In this first gentle act of courageousness, a change was launched, and her heart found love.

As time passed, Ivy held onto the bliss she felt in that initial experience and kept consistency within those prayerful moments. However, several months later, she realized the relationship was not fully formed. Still plagued with worry and doubt, these feelings forced Ivy to consider if she would be rejected and unloved. Knowing how important it was for their relationship, she shared this with Him. Together, they prayed with these feelings often, and one day while sitting in the quiet moments, a sense arose in her that this relationship mattered and she would have to fully surrender to enjoy its fruits.

One glorious day, Ivy welcomed that chance with open arms and let down every guard she had, thus allowing Him to have her heart. In doing so, their relationship blossomed and she grew confident in letting others see the boldness she had hidden away for so long. Ivy knew remaining honest with herself and through these experiences was crucial. She waited for the right moment and affectionately whispered, "God, I love you."

Ivy could not contain all she was feeling in the tenderness of this moment, and erupted in a prayerful discourse: "God, through your loving grace, I know You are the one who will always be there. You are my constant."

Through prayer and communication, authentic consolation was given, helping Ivy become who she was meant to be: "You have shown me what it is like to be open and honest. I never thought I could let another into my heart after what I went through, but You were there all along. Together through Scripture and prayer, a beacon of hope has illuminated my soul. Loving God, I offer You the thoughts from my mind, the words from my lips, and the desires of my heart, surrendering my own expectations for the grace which is Your love."

As time passed, Ivy was grateful for the turmoil she endured, knowing it as a means to the origin of her courage and confidence in herself as well as renewed companionship with God. Ivy often reflects back to the day she took a chance and God showed Himself to her. Through it all God brought her into His arms and held her tightly. She will be forever grateful that she opened herself to God's invitation, inspiring her to find the faith she needed to become rich with His spirit. Today, Ivy joins many others who have not only found their courageous voice but have also discovered the truth in God's Word.

– 27 –

Born First of Love
Janelle Roselli

I will not despair amidst the chaos.

I cannot cower in the face of anxiety.

I must stand firm,

But I must stand with peace.

For what good is hope

Hidden beneath the frailty of pride?

Dare we impose our rage upon the world

Just to cover the fear of our fragility?

Janelle Roselli

Instead, let us:
Seek the soul behind each story.
March into the flames of discord.
Quench the indignation of discomfort.

Let us:
Step into the depths of suffering
Walking alongside one another
With empathy and compassion.

Let us:
Hold fast
To the promise of Good
When there seems no other certainty to grasp.

Good promises:
When I am weak, then I am strong
And
The meek shall inherit the earth.

If this is indeed
The Land of the Free and the Home of the Brave
Should not our courage reflect the One
Who Conquered the Grave?

Born First of Love

If we proclaim
In God We Trust
Should not our actions be
Born first of Love?

Index of Authors

Barr, Janet M. 15
Celovsky, Debra 155
Cole-Kelly, Carlitta 101
Gray, Damon J. 59
Hagion, Christine 67
Hellard-Brown, Terrie 57
Hightower, Joyce Dixon 3
Juliusson, Elaine 49
Krause, Margaux 35
La Shay, Lainey 27
Lindsey, Lenette 147
Mackinnon, Malcolm 19, 131
Miller, Robynne Elizabeth 77
Mitchell, Rebecca 159
Mulder, Robyn 11
Novak, Kimberly 167
Peluso, Anita 45
Popish, Heather 75, 117
Roselli, Janelle 173
Schock, Darcy 109
Taylor-Worden, Libby 125
Warren, Debbie Jones 139
Weinberg, D.H. 85
Weisman, Michele Marie 119
Wood, Karen D. 93

Meet the Authors

Janet Barr

Since 2017, Janet has had to check the box marked "widow" on forms. Her husband, Steve, left her with an amazing family and many tasks that looked easy when he did them. Her poems generally start with journaling and prayers until the words start looking for a rhyme scheme.

Debra Celovsky

Debra has served in pastoral ministry with her husband for most of her adult life. She holds a B.A. in English Literature and her devotionals and articles have appeared in numerous publications. Debra is on the board of Inspire Christian Writers and Chair of the Editorial Team for the Inspire Anthology. She blogs through the One Year Bible at debracelovsky.com

Carlitta Cole-Kelly

Carlitta is a retired nurse who enjoys crafts, photography, and writing short non-fiction pieces and devotionals. Her work has appeared in the Upper Room Magazine, the American River College Literary Review Magazine, Christmas Moments, and the Inspire Forgiveness Anthology. She has one self-published children's book, *A Christmas Conversation: The Day Jesus Visited Santa*, and is working on a collection of true short stories about the many ways we can hear God in our everyday lives.

Damon Gray

Damon is a writer, speaker, husband, father, grandfather, former pastor, and member of the Inspire Board of Directors. Damon pursues his passion for teaching, making disciples, and advancing the kingdom of Jesus Christ by calling on men and women to embrace Long-View Living in a Short-View World.

Christine Hagion

Christine is an ordained minister, counselor, author, speaker, and advocate. A survivor herself, she has worked with victims and survivors of abuse for 20+ years, and her work reflects the wisdom she's gained from her clients. Known as "Dr. Red," she seeks to raise awareness about family violence at RevRedPhD.com.

Terrie Hellard-Brown

Terrie writes devotionals and children's stories. Her podcast, *Books that Spark*, reviews books that lead to teachable moments with our kids. Her blog discusses being Christ's disciple while discipling our children. Terrie uses her experiences as a mother, missionary, minister, and teacher to speak to the hearts of readers.

Joyce Dixon Hightower

Joyce writes to inspire Christians in the practical living out of belief. Her writings reflect her love of music and worldwide travel, and draw lessons from her experience as a medical provider and a single mother of three. She enjoys being Grandma, and is director of The Dixon-Hightower, Inc., which oversees projects for orphans.

Elaine Juliusson

Elaine writes Romance Adventure and Slice of Life stories. She draws story concepts from ranching, travel, and past client counseling experiences. She is active in her community and church. She lives in Loomis, California surrounded by incorrigible animals and two chatty daughters.

Margaux Krause

Margaux is author of the blog, *A Momma and Her Flock*, and her follow-up book, *Feeling like a Mom Devotional*. She enjoys being a stay-at-home mom to her two toddler daughters and wife to her husband, John. Together, the family likes to swim and play board games.

Lainey La Shay

Lainey writes to explore the deep and often difficult aspects of life and shines hope and courage into the lives of her readers. She loves to travel, explore, and spend time in God's creation.

Lenette Lindsey

Lenette is a Bible teacher, writer, and graduate from Dallas Theological Seminary who deeply loves Jesus and people. She lives in Texas with her husband, Joel. They recently became empty-nesters, except for Charlie, her angel in a doggie costume, and Sophie, who hasn't yet earned her wings.

Malcolm Mackinnon

Originally from England, Malcolm is a children's pastor, designer, and presenter. He is husband to Donna and dad to Jonathan (11) and Asiya (9). He writes in diverse genres including speculative fiction, devotionals, and sitcom scripts. Malcolm has lived in the Bay Area of California since 2011.

Robynne Elizabeth Miller, MFA

Robynne holds a B.A. in English Lit and an MFA in Creative Nonfiction/Fiction. She's wife to a Brit and mom to a brood of amazing kids. Ten books and multiple anthologies, collaborations, and countless articles/essays into her career, she's a writing/publishing coach, substantive editor, speaker, mentor, Inspire's president, and Director of the Vision Christian Writers Conference at Mt. Hermon. Her passion is equipping and encouraging writers. www.robynnemiller.com

Rebecca Mitchell

Rebecca is a lecturer at University of California, Davis, co-leader of DivorceCare at Bayside Church, and mother of two beautiful adult daughters. Her book, *From Broken Vows to Healed Hearts: Seeking God After Divorce Through Community, Scripture, and Journaling*, brings hope to wounded hearts.

Robyn Mulder

Robyn lives in South Dakota. Her husband became a pastor after farming for many years. They have four grown children and one adorable grandson (so far!). Robyn writes about mental health, faith, and perseverance (among other things) at robynmulder.com.

Kimberly Novak

Kimberly is a wife, mother, author, and Spiritual Director. Her passion for inspiring those on a spiritual journey has bloomed into various ministries. Kimberly's mission is to enhance each journey by guiding others where the light of strength is God's love. Her blog and writings are at kimberlynovak.com.

Anita Peluso

Anita is a quilter and amateur hobby farmer who fell into writing devotionals for social media. She lives in Western Washington with her husband, two cats, four ducks, and five chickens.

Heather J. Popish

Heather lives with her husband and young children in the Sacramento, California area. She enjoys working as a freelance editor and encouraging others through her writing. Previously published in *Inspire Grace*, you can read more of her writing at hpopish.wordpress.com.

Janelle Roselli

Janelle is a YA Fantasy writer with a passion for helping young adults cope with real life situations by processing them through fictional story. When not writing Janelle can be found mentoring junior high and high school students, walking her two rescue dogs, or golfing with her husband.

Darcy Schock

Darcy writes heartfelt words that push back the darkness so the light of hope, peace, and happiness can shine. She blogs and shares updates on the historical fiction novel she's writing at darcyschock.com. Darcy resides in central Illinois with her husband and three daughters.

Libby Taylor-Worden

Libby is the author of women's fiction set against the backdrop of the motorcycle culture. She lives in Northern California with her husband where she is engaged in women's ministry within the outlaw motorcycle world.

Debbie Jones Warren

Born in Alameda, California, Debbie Jones Warren moved to Nigeria with her missionary parents before her first birthday. Now in Castro Valley, California, she and her husband, Chris, love time with their three adult children and their daughter-in-love. Debbie enjoys cooking gluten-free, learning German, and hosting garden teas for friends.

D.H. Weinberg

D.H. loves God, history, suspense, and books where you learn something. Thus, he writes thrillers, inspirational, and historical fiction from those perspectives.

Michele Marie Weisman

Michele, published in the Inspire Kindness Anthology, blogs weekly at *Walking on Mustard Seeds*. A California native, she and her family recently settled in the heart of Texas. A walk to the lake is her favorite way to start the day, followed by a cup of coffee with her husband.

Karen D. Wood

Karen received a B.A. in Fine Arts, a Master of Social Work (MSW), and is a Licensed Clinical Social Worker with a Neurotherapy practice. She is author of *Brain Prayers: Explore Your Brain, Expand Your Prayers*. Karen has finished a similar book for children and is working on a new book, *Grief and the Brain*.

About Inspire Christian Writers

Inspire Christian Writers is a nonprofit organization whose sole reason for existing is to equip and encourage writers, no matter where you are in your writing career. Started in California, Inspire now has members from multiple countries and across the US. And what was begun as a simple writing group has developed into a comprehensive organization meeting the needs of writers in numerous ways:

- Our award-winning blog and website, (named a top ten world-wide resource for Christian writers!)
- Online and in-person critique groups
- Writing Contests
- Directory of vetted professionals serving writers, with discounts!
- Workshops, both in-person and online
- Networking opportunities
- Writing credits (via our blog, contests, anthology, etc.)
- Discounts for members to some conferences, events, and contests
- Annual anthology
- And the Vision Christian Writers conference at Mt. Hermon (vcwconf.com ... with a discount larger than Inspire's annual membership fee.)

If you are interested in joining Inspire, or want information on our current events and offerings, please visit www.inspirewriters.com.

We look forward to welcoming you into our family!

Previous Anthologies from Inspire Christian Writers

Inspire Trust (2012)

Inspire Faith (2013)

Friends of Inspire Faith (2013)

Inspired Glimpses of God's Presence (2013)

Inspire Victory (2014)

Inspire Promise (2014)

Inspire Forgiveness (2015)

Inspire Joy (2016)

Inspire Love (2017)

Inspire Kindness (2018)

Inspire Grace (2019)

Inspire Community (2021)

Made in the USA
Monee, IL
03 January 2023